Using
Performance
Measurement
to Improve
Outcomes
in Ambulatory Care

JOINT COMMISSION

Joint Commission Mission
The mission of the Joint Commission on Accreditation of Healthcare Organizations is to improve the quality of care provided to the public through the provision of health care accreditation and related services that support performance improvement in health care organizations.

Joint Commission educational programs and publications support, but are separate from, the accreditation activities of the Joint Commission. Attendees at Joint Commission educational programs and purchasers of Joint Commission publications receive no special consideration or treatment in, or confidential information about, the accreditation process.

Printed in the U.S.A. 5 4 3 2 1

Requests for permission to reprint or make copies of any part of this book should be addressed to:
Permissions Editor
Joint Commission on Accreditation of Healthcare Organizations
One Renaissance Boulevard
Oakbrook Terrace, IL 60181

ISBN: 0-86688-603-6
Library of Congress Catalog Number: 98-87970

For more information about the Joint Commission, please visit our Web site at http://www.jcaho.org.

CONTENTS

INTRODUCTION

Health care performance measurement is an evolving science, informed by past experience and driven by emerging information needs. The goal of performance measurement in ambulatory care is to accurately understand the cause of current performance so that better results can be achieved through focused improvement actions.

The Search to Discover and Provide the Best Care

Outcomes management originates from the complex search for the best health care and how to provide it. Professional literature describes many ways to manage a plethora of clinical ailments (such as asthma, diabetes, hypertension, and congestive heart failure) in varying, and often contradictory detail. Authors seek to convince readers that a particular health plan, service model, or treatment approach is more clinically effective and cost-efficient than alternatives. They further describe the evolution of ambulatory health care and the vast number of services and treatments provided. Through the development of clinical pathways and the defining of care standards in outcomes management, guidelines are provided for the delivery and assessment of clinical care interventions for a variety of diseases and care needs.

Practitioners question the impact of their work. Administrators question the effectiveness and efficiency of their organization. Does the delivered treatment make a real difference in the patient's life? Does the patient get better? Get well? Can the patient return to normal daily activities? Is the ambulatory care organization, as it presently operates, viable? Is the current care system capable of fostering meaningful improvement? Does the treatment effect warrant the treatment cost? Do interventions lead to unwanted effects? What are the consequences of not providing treatment?

Professionals in ambulatory care settings continue to ask these compelling questions. Concerns about the benefits, value, and reliability of treatment and service models are the foundation of contemporary outcomes measurement in ambulatory health care.

Health care researchers and performance improvement professionals conduct a variety of investigative initiatives to understand the ramifications of alternative treatment settings, the effects of different medications, and the impact of various therapeutic interventions. The purpose of these studies is to explicate the complex relationships among a multitude of patient-focused, practitioner-centered, and treatment-related variables. This understanding can then lead to the formulation of care models that are most likely to produce desirable results and avoid unwanted outcomes. This is outcomes research—the search for best practices.

Why measure performance? Why measure outcomes? To discover, demonstrate, and make available the best possible ambulatory health care services at the least possible expense. No other performance improvement goal is more important.

The current health care environment is rich with resources to aid in meaningful performance measurement. Now is the time for delivery organizations to employ measures and measurement systems to objectively evaluate the efficacy of provided treatment. Only then can the multiple performance information demands of various stakeholders be addressed.

The Origins of Performance Measurement in Health Care

The roots of performance measurement and improvement are embedded in the history and evolution of health care. Early practitioners like Florence Nightingale, Ignaz Semmelweis, and Joseph Lister became outcomes researchers spontaneously. They were compelled to respond to nagging questions about whether contemporary treatment approaches helped the sick regain health.[1,2]

In the early 1900s Ernest Codman, himself a surgeon, recommended that surgeons systematically collect, review, and publicize data about the outcomes of their surgical interventions. He was publicly chastised for this then-unpopular viewpoint and was ultimately forced out of the medical profession. Today, however, many recognize Ernest Codman as the "father" of health care outcomes measurement.[3]

The Origins of Outcomes Management in Health Care

The beginning of the outcomes management movement can be traced to the work of John Wennberg, an epidemiologist, and his colleague Alan Gittlesohn. In 1972 they examined discharge data from all hospitals in Vermont and discovered large and unexplained variations in rates of several common surgeries. Their research led to the discovery that the likelihood of having surgery had more to do with where an individual lived than what their clinical status was.[4] This information fueled a growing interest in understanding the contributors to achieved outcomes. If understood, these critical contributory factors could then be manipulated to enhance the accomplishment of the desired end result.

As health care costs escalated and the need for health care reform became more pressing, the notion of outcomes management as a way to actively control both health care delivery and patient and organization results became increasingly appealing. From a clinical perspective, outcomes represent the patient's overall health status, including physical, psychological, functional, and interpersonal or social health. From a business perspective, outcomes represent the nonclinical aspects of organization performance. These include resources used, costs, degree of satisfaction, patient loyalty (that is, returning to the organization for future health care needs), judgements about the value and quality of the episode of care, and the likelihood that a patient will recommend the organization and its practitioners to family and friends. Not surprisingly, health care providers (clinicians and administrators), and others (patients, purchasers, payers, accreditors, and

regulators), began to think about achieved outcomes as evidence of treatment efficacy and organization effectiveness and efficiency.

The Current Status of Outcomes Management

Outcomes management is commonly viewed as a strategy for directly improving patient outcomes. Achieved outcomes are related to implemented processes. Specifically, this relationship suggests that results can be altered by changing the process(es) that produces them. As such, the term *outcomes management* is a misnomer because outcomes themselves are not managed; rather, the process that leads to the outcome(s) of interest is managed.[5]

Today, many view outcomes management as a strategy for designing and delivering services in a way that optimizes the desired results, while simultaneously reducing unnecessary resource consumption.[6] Meaningful outcomes management is fundamentally a research endeavor based on the collection and interpretation of performance data. Once collected, these performance data are used to understand *how* the current outcomes are achieved. Based on this understanding, alternative ways to achieve the same or better outcomes can be systematically and objectively tested, evaluated, and implemented.

Two major types of contemporary outcomes research exist. The first, often conducted using stringent research approaches, is evaluation of medical care effectiveness. The second, evaluation of health care quality, is an applied science that is focused on rapidly identifying and systematically testing different care processes in clinical settings. Ultimately, both are conducted for performance improvement purposes.

The Agency for Health Care Policy and Research (AHCPR) of the United States Public Health Service oversees research that assesses the effectiveness of medical treatment. AHCPR is particularly interested in the short- and long-term effects of specific treatments on achieving multiple outcomes.

The flourishing interest in maximizing the value of health care has fueled the performance improvement movement. Performance assessment examines patterns of care delivery in an attempt to optimize patient well-being and increase consumer satisfaction. One goal of outcomes measurement is to discover and define the patterns of care that consistently yield the most desirable outcomes. Such outcomes include the best clinical results and a minimal consumption of resources.[7]

The Need for Outcomes Measurement in Ambulatory Care

A variety of factors contribute to the reasons why ambulatory care organizations engage in outcomes measurement. All of them are anchored in the need for data—data that may be used for multiple purposes. Patients and consumer advocacy groups demand clear, understandable information about what results can be realistically achieved from different treatments, organizations, and providers. Armed with such information, patients can make rational and informed decisions regarding their treatment and care. Purchasers are persistently seeking explanations for variations in health care outcomes. Examination of differences across organizations, services, and practitioners leads to the selection of health care providers and the design of benefits packages. Payers and managed care providers are requesting cost/benefit data. Comparing the degree of patient improvement to the cost for the level/intensity of care delivered is central to developing reimbursement structures. Various oversight bodies now require data demonstrating improvement in both clinical and organization outcomes. Such information is becoming a more significant factor in the decision to award licensure or accreditation.[7]

These factors encourage ambulatory care organizations to engage in outcomes measurement. The demands for data will not diminish. In fact, such demands are likely to increase. This imperative for objective performance measurement and assessment forms the backdrop for this book.

Benefits from Performance Measurement

Patients may not be aware of the performance measurement initiatives conducted at the ambulatory care organization where they receive care. However, they often experience the results of those activities. The care they receive may be more appropriate and effective. The essential services they need may be more readily available and accessible. Their treatment episode may be more fluid and integrated across different practitioners and diagnostics. Their care may be simultaneously comprehensive and cost-effective. They may believe they are consistently treated with dignity and respect. These are some of the most meaningful benefits of performance measurement.

Performance measurement benefits the health care delivery organization as well. Ongoing, reliable, and valid measurement generates performance information that allows the provider organization to

■ have continuous access to objective data that support ongoing quality improvement;

■ receive and respond to early warnings of performance improvement opportunities;

■ verify the effectiveness of corrective actions;

■ highlight areas of outstanding performance; and

■ compare their performance to that of peer organizations using the same measures within the same performance measurement system.[8]

Effective performance measurement produces descriptive data and information that the ambulatory care organization can use to

■ judge the stability and predictability of existing processes;

■ identify the need for improvement through the redesign of existing processes; and

■ determine the need for the design of new processes.

In addition, data generated through performance measurement activities highlight actual performance in high impact areas. These data can then be used to help the organization's leadership identify strategic performance improvement goals. In this way, performance measurement becomes integral to an organization's strategic planning process. Furthermore, the ongoing collection of strategic performance data provides a picture of the organization's performance over time.

Performance measurement benefits purchasers by providing evidence of the efficacy, appropriateness, and cost-effectiveness of different service delivery models and treatment approaches. This information allows for more informed decision making and selection of benefits.

Payers also benefit from performance measurement by better projecting the total expense of care, both within and across various health plans and levels of service.

Accreditors and regulators benefit from performance measurement by gaining more access to information about an ambulatory care organization's actual performance. Evidence of how care is provided and the subsequent outcomes achieved illustrates how well an organization is performing.

The Joint Commission and the Evolution of Performance Measurement

The Joint Commission's fifty-year mission to improve the quality of health care has been actualized through an accreditation process characterized by an on-site, standards-based organization evaluation. This assessment of standards compliance produces useful but incomplete information. Data about achieved results are lacking. Consequently, interest in measuring, assessing, and monitoring performance—the actual results of care—has grown. Focusing on results is no substitute for evaluating standards compliance. Both are vital; they complement each other and provide an integrated evaluation of organization performance that is more accurate and thorough than either approach would be alone.[9]

Responding to this need to evaluate achieved performance comprehensively, in 1986 the Joint Commission launched the Agenda for Change,

a multiyear, multiphased modernization of the accreditation process. Three major initiatives drove the effort.

First, Joint Commission standards were rewritten, strongly emphasizing the interdependent nature of all critical functions (for example, patient-focused functions and organization functions) within a health care organization. Furthermore, the revised standards focused much less on what an organization was capable of doing and much more on the outcomes an organization actually achieved.

Second, the requirement for regular and systematic performance measurement—measurement of clinical and nonclinical outcomes and processes—was intensified. Once such outcomes and process data were available, organization performance could be systematically evaluated from two perspectives: the organization's historical performance over time and its performance in comparison to similar organizations.

Finally, the creation of a more performance-oriented accreditation process led to revisions in on-site, pre- and post-survey activities. Consumers of services and staff from all levels within the organization became more integrally involved in the survey visit. And organizations seeking accreditation became much more focused on demonstrating the analysis and improvement of outcomes of care.

The Joint Commission's ORYX Initiative

In time, all organizations seeking Joint Commission accreditation will be required to continue to comply with applicable standards, including those that address the need to measure key organization structures, processes, and outcomes. In addition, organizations must continue to use *performance measurement* as a way to continuously evaluate their performance and foster process and outcome improvement. Over time, the required use of *performance measurement systems* will be integrated into the accreditation process. To be useful, such measurement systems must offer flexibility and choice of specific measures and measurements.

As originally contemplated by the Agenda for Change, these anticipated performance measurement requirements will include

- systematic collection, comparison, and analysis of data on the health care organization's performance;
- representative measurement of the health care services provided by each organization, using appropriate methods to account for variations in their specific patient populations; and
- use of acceptable *performance measurement systems* and measures.[10]

A core component of the Joint Commission's Agenda for Change, this evolution of performance measurement is currently known as the ORYX initiative.

The Joint Commission anticipates numerous benefits from integrating performance measurement into the accreditation process. It is expected that this integration will

- enhance the value of accreditation by linking it with outcomes of care;
- strengthen the accreditation decision by making it more credible, objective, consistent, and useful;
- increase reliance on Joint Commission accreditation, further supporting the consensus development of standards and performance measures and decreasing the need for duplicative organization evaluation activities; and
- generate performance data that the Joint Commission can use to
  - continuously monitor organization performance;
  - assist organizations in identifying areas in need of attention;
  - focus on-site, triennial surveys on areas that afford the greatest opportunities for improvement;
  - facilitate benchmarking by identifying exemplary performance and best practices;
  - foster refinement of performance-based standards; and

  - explicate the relationships between standards and outcomes.

Organization of this Book

This book is divided into seven chapters and an appendix. Chapter 1 summarizes the basic information that is essential for a solid understanding of performance and outcomes measurement in ambulatory care. Chapter 2 describes what organizations must do to commit to ongoing performance measurement and improvement. Chapter 3 focuses on measures that are pertinent to ambulatory care settings. Chapter 4 explores the Joint Commission's perspective on the use of performance measurement systems. Chapter 5 offers practical advice on how to conduct an outcomes measurement project. Chapter 6 provides a self-directed learning exercise on designing an outcomes measurement project. Chapter 7 provides case stories from two different organizations, showcasing real outcomes measurement studies. The appendix includes a series of worksheets designed to help transfer key concepts into practice environments. A glossary defines many of the terms used throughout this book.

Use of this Book

Several learning aids, which can be used independently or in groups, are included in this book. *Thought Breaks* are a series of focusing questions to clarify the importance of performance measurement and improvement concepts to ambulatory care organizations. *Exercise Breaks* are the basis to complete worksheets in the Appendix that offer a structured approach to clarifying and conducting performance measurement initiatives in practice environments. The self-directed learning exercise offers the challenge of assuming a consultant's role and developing an outcomes measurement effort for a fictitious ambulatory care clinic.

Practicing clinicians, managers, leaders, and performance improvement specialists working in any ambulatory care setting can use this book as a performance and outcomes measurement reference. It can be a learning aid for staff education about performance improvement. It can serve as a practical guide when implementing performance and outcomes measurement projects. Both undergraduate and graduate-level students may find this book helpful as a practical summary on the application of performance measurement techniques in service/care delivery environments.

Acknowledgments

This book is the result of the efforts of many people. Gratitude is expressed to the individuals who brought an extensive knowledge of ambulatory care, performance improvement, and performance measurement to the critical review of this manuscript. Your time and thoughtful comments are deeply appreciated.

The dedicated professionals at the case story organizations willingly agreed to help us learn through their performance improvement experiences. Your hard work demonstrates the translation of quality and performance theory into real practice. Many thanks are offered to Colonel Robert M. Saad, MD, Commander, 59 Medical Operations Squadron; Major Sandra A. Black, BSN, Nurse Manager, Division of Cardiology; and Salvadore Dominguez, Superintendent, 59 Medical Operations Squadron from Wilford Hall Medical Center. We further thank Nancy Kowal, MS, RNC, MP, Manager, Pain Service and Chair, Ambulatory Clinical Management Group and Donald Stevens, MD, Unit Chief—Pain Service, from the University of Massachusetts Medical Center. The time and effort you gave to this project are very much appreciated.

We would also like to thank those who reviewed this manuscript in its various stages. These reviewers' comments have been most helpful. The reviewers include Carol A. Jones-Wright, RN, MBA, Chief Planning and Development Officer, Central North Alabama Health Services, Inc., Huntsville, Alabama; Maureen Keating, Pediatric Outpatient Center, Hackensack University Medical Center, Hackensack, New Jersey; Sandra W. Pearson, Nurse Manager, Tuckahoe Surgery Center, Richmond, Virginia; Christine Peterson, MD, Department of Student Health, University of Virginia in Charlottesville; and Sandra Pollack, RN, Director of Family Practice Center, Riverside Regional Medical Center/Riverside Health System, Newport News, Virginia.

Thanks are extended to Diane Cesarone for her efforts in writing this book. Diane's expertise and dedication have enhanced the value of this publication. We truly appreciate her contribution.

Finally, deep gratitude is expressed to you, the reader. Your commitment to the patients entrusted in your care is reflected in your dedication to ongoing learning and continuous improvement of the quality of the health services you provide each day.

References

1.   Lang N: Nurses are involved "closely and constantly" in quality of care. *Health Management Quarterly* pp 10–13, Jan–Apr 1987.

2.   Wenzel RP: *Prevention and Control of Nosocomial Infections.* Baltimore: Williams & Wilkins, 1927.

3.   Joint Commission on Accreditation of Healthcare Organizations: *The Measurement Mandate.* Oakbrook Terrace, IL, 1993.

4.   Outcomes management comes of age. (Special Report.) *Business and Health* 14(suppl B):7–10, Apr 1996.

5.   Nadzam DM: Nurses and the measurement of health care: An overview. In Joint Commission on Accreditation of Healthcare Organizations. *Nursing Practice and Outcomes Measurement.* Oakbrook Terrace, IL, 1997, p 7.

6.   Ortmeier BG: Conducting clinical and health economic outcome studies in an ambulatory setting. *JAMA* 20(4):10–16, October 1997.

7.   Wilkins EG, Lowery JC, Smith DJ: Outcomes research: A primer for plastic surgeons. *Annals of Plastic Surgery* 37(1):1–11, July 1996.

8.   Joint Commission on Accreditation of Healthcare Organizations: *1998–99 Comprehensive Accreditation Manual for Ambulatory Care.* Oakbrook Terrace, IL, 1998.

9.   Loeb JM, O'Leary DS: From the Joint Commission on Accreditation of Healthcare Organizations. *JAMA* 273(18):1405, May 1995.

10. Seidenfeld J, Hanold LS, Loeb JM: From the Joint Commission on Accreditation of Healthcare Organizations. *JAMA* 273(9):691, March 1995.

Chapter 1:

Performance Measurement in Ambulatory Care

This chapter does the following:

1. Explores the relationship between processes and outcomes;

2. Compares the clinical care process to the process of organization improvement;

3. Enumerates three types of measures;

4. Identifies three purposes for performance measurement;

5. Highlights performance measurement as a tool for improving performance;

6. Lists the characteristics of effective measurement; and

7. Enumerates the benefits of outcomes measurement.

The Relationship Between Processes and Outcomes: The Linchpin of Effective Performance Measurement

Meaningful performance measurement and significant performance improvement are grounded in the inherent relationship between processes and outcomes. A process is an interrelated series of events, activities, actions, mechanisms, or steps that transform inputs into outputs. Outcomes are the result of the performance or nonperformance of a process or processes. To understand processes and outcomes in ways that are meaningful for performance improvement, they should not be stripped of this relational context. Indeed, successful performance improvement is contingent upon being both outcomes oriented and process minded.

Being outcomes oriented means continuously keeping the desired future result for a specific patient or group of patients within the visual field. Being process minded means not losing sight of the predictable, and occasionally unpredictable, interactions of the key actions, decisions, and judgments that produce those desired results. Perhaps a simple analogy captures this complex dynamic. Outcomes are the destination—the journey's end. Processes are the roadmaps that guide us and the vehicles that transport us from where we are to where we wish to be.

Performance improvement in ambulatory care challenges us to measure and assess key processes and related outcomes at multiple levels. We should continually answer the following questions:

1. What are the actual and desired outcomes for the individual patient? What processes contribute to these outcomes?

2. What are the actual and desired outcomes for patients with common characteristics

Table 1-1. Comparison of the Clinical Care and Organization Improvement Processes

Clinical Care Process	Organization Improvement Process
Assess clinical status.	Assess current organization performance.
Diagnose and identify needs.	Identify and prioritize areas for improvement.
Develop treatment plan.	Develop strategic and operational improvement plans.
Implement interventions.	Implement improvement actions.
Evaluate clinical status.	Evaluate organization performance.

(for example, gender, age, ethnicity, socio-economic status, geographic location, work history, and so forth)? What processes contribute to these outcomes?

3. What are the actual and desired outcomes for patients with common diagnoses and therapeutic interventions? What processes contribute to these outcomes?

4. What are the actual and desired outcomes for patients with common diagnoses and different therapeutic interventions? What processes contribute to these outcomes?

5. What are the actual and desired outcomes for patients receiving care (treatment or diagnosis) in a common setting? What processes contribute to these outcomes?

6. What are the actual and desired outcomes for individual patients and groups of patients who are treated by different practitioners?

These questions can only be answered correctly and confidently when the processes that yield such outcomes have been identified, described, measured, and assessed.

Experienced practitioners understand the process-outcome relationship "intuitively." In fact, the provision of clinical care is predicated on this process-outcome dynamic. Assessing the patient's condition initiates the planning of individualized, scientifically sound treatment. Next, the desired outcomes, the treatment goals for the individual, are identified. A variety of

interventional strategies are considered, and the staff providing care and services use their experience and knowledge to formulate the individualized plan of care. The treatment plan is documented, interventions are implemented, and care is provided. The patient's progress toward goals achievement is analyzed, the outcomes of the provided treatment are evaluated, and the therapeutic interventions are revised in accordance with the individual's changing health status. This cycle continues until the patient leaves the health care system or is transferred to another level of care.

Providing care and services in this fashion is to be outcomes oriented and process minded—reflecting a deep knowledge of the powerful relationship between processes and outcomes. This understanding can be broadened and applied to strategically improving the performance of an organization or any of its elements. Table 1-1, above, illustrates the similarities between the clinical care process and the organization improvement process.

THOUGHT BREAK

■ *Take a few moments to consider the relationship between processes and outcomes.*

■ *Review the key clinical outcomes your ambulatory care organization strives to achieve.*

■ *Review also the important outcomes you strive to achieve when caring for patient populations and individual patients.*

■ *Try to identify all the major processes that relate to each of these outcomes.*

■ *Think about how consistently the processes you have identified lead to the desired results.*

■ *Begin to generate some initial hypotheses about why these processes may or may not contribute to the achievement of the desired outcomes.*

Types of Measures

There are three components of quality: structure, process, and outcome. Meaningful measures can be developed for each of these components. Structures describe the organization system's characteristics, such as structure, specialty mix, workload, and financial incentives; provider demographics and traits; and patient demographics, including health habits, beliefs, and preferences. Structure measures capture data about elemental aspects of the organization that must be present for it to operate and provide service(s). Processes include the technical aspects of care, including number of patient visits and encounters, prescribed medications and other treatments, referrals, diagnostics, hospitalizations, and continuity or coordination of care. Processes also include interpersonal care styles including the provider's interactional approaches, counseling, and teaching; and the patient's degree of participation in care processes. Processes additionally include those nonclinical activities that support the organization's day-to-day operations. Process measures collect data on various dimensions of clinical and nonclinical work activities. Clinical outcomes are multidimensional and describe the results from the delivery of care. Business results include such outcomes as expense/revenue ratios, patient and staff satisfaction, productivity, and throughput. Outcome measures acquire data about the achieved results of clinical and nonclinical work.[1] See Table 1-2, page 4, for examples of structure, process, and outcomes measures pertinent to ambulatory care settings.

Structure measures typically evaluate an organization's capability to provide quality care and services. They generally do not reveal information about real performance. In contrast, process and outcomes measures usually generate data that describe actual performance. That is why ambulatory care organizations frequently allocate more measurement resources to the collection and analysis of process and outcomes data than to the collection and analysis of structure data.

EXERCISE BREAK

Take a few moments to complete Worksheet #1: Types of Performance Measures, which is on page 132 in the Appendix. Part I will help you draft operational definitions for structure, process, and outcome measures that will be meaningful for your own ambulatory care organization. Part II will help you list examples of important structures, processes, and outcomes that are present in your own organization. You may also find the completion of this worksheet to be a useful component of a performance measurement effort.

Purposes of Measurement

Traditional quality improvement literature identifies three fundamental purposes for conducting performance measurement: assessment of current performance, demonstration and verification of performance improvement, and control of performance.

Assessment of Current Performance

Conventional wisdom tells us that if baseline performance data are lacking, it is impossible to know if improvement has occurred. Therefore, measurement to assess performance is often a first step in a structured performance improvement project. Such measurement produces data that illustrate the strengths and weaknesses of current process operations and achieved outcomes.

Table 1-2. Examples of Structures, Processes, and Outcomes in Ambulatory Care Settings

Structures:
1. A defined medication recall system
2. Competency checklists that demonstrate staff skills and abilities
3. Accepted definitions of the patient information that is necessary for determining the appropriate care setting
4. Properly functioning equipment
5. Adequate availability of supplies

Processes:
6. Conducting an initial physical and psychosocial assessment and health history for each patient
7. Obtaining informed consent
8. Assessment of the patient's values, abilities, learning needs, and readiness to learn
9. Multidisciplinary approach to providing care
10. Coordination of care across settings and among practitioners
11. Resolution of denials of care
12. Billing
13. Scheduling of appointments

Outcomes:
14. Symptom remission
15. Patient adherence to therapeutic prescriptions (for example, medications, diet, exercise regimen, and so forth)
16. Number and percent of patient's functional days (days at school or work)
17. Wait time from first contact to first appointment
18. Occurrences of denied payment
19. Completeness and accuracy of medical records
20. Occurrences of hazardous materials exposures
21. Percent of new and returning patients
22. Number and type of patients seen, by practitioner

Demonstration and Verification of Performance Improvement

Another purpose of measurement is to illustrate performance improvement objectively. Validating improvement by "gut impression" or "intuition" is inadequate. A factual picture of performance can be provided by examining how changes affect processes and outcomes. In this way, measuring for improvement strives to show that process performance or achieved results are improved (in one or more ways) as a consequence of making changes to the process.

Control of Performance

A final reason for measurement is to control performance. Measures for control compose an "early warning and correction system." When it occurs, the early warning system highlights an undesirable change in process operations. The correction system delineates specific actions that should be taken in response to particular process deviations. Measures for control, therefore, identify the deviation in real time and enable an immediate correction to be made.

Often, although not always, the same or similar measures may be used for different purposes (assessment, improvement, or control). Table 1-3, page 5, offers examples of measures that may be used for assessment, improvement, and control purposes in ambulatory health care settings.

Table 1-3. Examples of Measures That Can Be Used for Assessment, Improvement, and Control Purposes

Assessment (measures that assess baseline performance):

1. Undocumented medical histories (total number and percentage of undocumented medical histories per individual patient in the correctional health center, ongoing collection)
2. Referral sources for admission to the dialysis center (name and number of referrals from each source for the preceding six months)
3. Missed school for children and adolescents because of physical therapy appointments (number of hours of school missed because of conflicting physical therapy appointments for the previous quarter)
4. Utilization of student health center (number of students seeking initial and repeat service at the student health center, ongoing collection)
5. Experienced pain (number and intensity of pain episodes during the past week)

Improvement (measures that illustrate change following the implementation of improvement activities):

6. Timely initiation of chemotherapy following redesign of the medication administration protocols and staff education (number, percentage, and reason for delays in initiating chemotherapy for the past two months and the subsequent two months)
7. Percentage of clients keeping mammography appointments after receiving a written appointment schedule from the women's health center (percentage of patients who received mammograms as scheduled for the previous quarter and the next)
8. Number of and reasons for missed appointments in the Veteran's Affairs clinics following the initiation of telephone reminder calls (percentage of patients who failed to attend scheduled appointments for the quarter before the telephone reminder calls and ongoing collection after initiation of the calls)
9. Participation in immunization programs sponsored by the public health clinics following distribution of a pediatric care services brochure (percentage of families participating in the immunization program for the two quarters before and ongoing following distribution of the brochure)

Control (measures that include a corrective action to return deviating performance to acceptable levels):

10. Use of an established protocol for the administration of sedating medications to patients unable to complete MRI because of agitation (number and percent of patients receiving PRN sedating medications that are able to complete the MRI, ongoing collection)
11. Use of established guidelines for the administration of PRN oxygen to patients undergoing cardiac catheterization. Guidelines specify the lowest acceptable oxygen saturation level (92%) and the desired flow rate of the administered oxygen (number of cardiac catheterization patients receiving oxygen because of unacceptably low oxygen saturation; percent of patients receiving PRN oxygen whose saturation returns to acceptable levels, ongoing collection)
12. Use of physician-approved clinical assessment and intervention guidelines that define the level of consciousness and vital signs, indicating when to administer multiple doses of conscious sedation agents to patients undergoing sigmoidoscopy (percent of patients undergoing sigmoidoscopy who receive multiple doses of conscious sedation agents; level of consciousness and vital signs for patients receiving one, two, three, or more doses of conscious sedation, ongoing collection)
13. Adherence to manufacturer's guidelines to recalibrate finger-stick blood glucose monitors in the primary care office when test standard levels are higher or lower than tolerance limits (frequency of recalibration of blood glucose monitors, ongoing collection)

THOUGHT BREAK

- *Recall the purpose(s) of performance measurement at your ambulatory care organization.*

- *Review the performance measurement initiatives currently underway in your facility.*

- *Identify specific measures currently in use and determine the purpose(s) for each. Are they measures for assessment, improvement, or control?*

- *Evaluate whether your organization is conducting performance measurement for all three purposes. If not, begin to explore why not.*

- *Try to generate some suggestions for effectively and meaningfully using measures for assessment, improvement, and control at your organization.*

Performance Measurement as a Tool

Measurement should be employed as a tool, a means to explicate essential answers to compelling questions about organization performance. Meaningful performance measurement answers questions such as the following:

1. What does our organization do?
2. How well are we doing?
3. How have we done over time?
4. How do we compare to other organizations?
5. Why are we doing well in certain areas?
6. In what areas can we improve?
7. How can we achieve improvements in these areas?
8. How can we best serve our population of patients?

Characteristics of Effective Measurement

Measurement in ambulatory care settings requires knowledgeable staff, support for data management, and dedicated time. Given this rich investment, it is important that both process and outcomes measurement are conducted as effectively and efficiently as possible.

Reliability And Validity

For performance measurement to be effective, both the data collection tool(s) and the measures must be reliable and valid. They must generate accurate and complete data. Only then can the findings be studied, interpreted, and acted upon confidently.

Validity and reliability are attributes of measures and data collection instruments. Validity reflects appropriateness of data for the defined purpose. Valid measures identify opportunities for improvement and demonstrate actual progress in outcomes and the quality of care. Reliability refers to data constancy and consistency. Reliable measures accurately and consistently identify the events they were designed to identify across multiple health care settings.

Operational definitions of data elements should be created to ensure that all essential data are correctly and comprehensively captured. In order to determine face validity, subject matter experts should ensure that operational definitions make sense, are correct, and are complete.

Pilot testing each data collection instrument helps to ensure that performance data are collected and recorded consistently. A data collector can abstract the same patient records at different times. This evaluates test–retest reliability, meaning the same data collector consistently records the same data in the same way at different times. If more than one person collects data for a performance measurement project, the different data collectors can abstract the same patient record for the same data. This determines interrater reliability, which evaluates the degree to which different data collectors document the same data in the same way. Consistently high rates (80% or higher) of agreement in the way data are recorded demonstrates acceptable interrater reliability.

Relevance

Effective measurement must be relevant to the core work of the ambulatory care organization. It should be linked to the organization's mission, vision, values, and strategic goals and objectives. Data should be collected on high impact clinical and nonclinical processes and outcomes. When this occurs, performance measurement and improvement become an intrinsic part of the ambulatory care organization's core work.

Comprehensiveness

Effective measurement encompasses the full range of processes and outcomes within the organization. As such, performance measurement should include (but is not limited to)

- clinical processes and outcomes, including
  - assessment of patients,
  - care of patients,
  - education of patients,
  - surveillance, prevention, and control of infection, and
  - issues related to the continuum of care;
- administrative processes and outcomes, including
  - patient rights and organization ethics,
  - issues related to the management of the environment,
  - issues related to the management of human resources, and
  - information management;
- satisfaction of patients, staff, and other vested stakeholders;
- financial performance; and
- organization relationship in the community.

Variability

Variation is the range of performance that is present, to some extent, in all operationalized processes and achieved outcomes. Five major sources of variation in health care have been identified: patient factors, organization factors, staff factors, environmental factors, and chance.[2]

Performance improvement is grounded in an understanding of the type and magnitude of the variation that is present. There are two types of variation: common cause and special cause. Common cause variation occurs randomly and is an inherent part of every performance system (processes, functions, and organizations). The

reduction or elimination of common cause variation requires change in the system of performance itself. Special cause variation results from a specific assignable cause that is not inherent in the performance system, but can be identified. Special cause variation may produce undesirable or desirable effects. Reduction or elimination of undesired special cause variation is achieved by modifying or eliminating its cause. Integrating the cause of desirable special cause variation into normal process operations will lead to the consistent achievement of better outcomes.

When selecting improvement opportunities emergent from the measurement and assessment of variation, it is helpful to consider the magnitude of the variation. Wide-ranging variation and/or an average performance that significantly deviates from acceptable or desirable performance levels affords opportunities for high impact improvements. Narrower variation and/or average performance that is less deviant from desirable performance levels offers additional improvement opportunities.[3] Table 1-4, page 8, provides examples of common and special cause variation in ambulatory health care settings.

Usefulness

Effective measurement yields useful data that can be transformed into meaningful information that can be used to improve process operations and/or outcomes. Lawthers and Wood[4] offer sound guidance when they suggest that indicator data in an effective measurement activity should be related to patient care, associated with processes that can be altered, measured over time, applied within and across organizations, quantified, and risk adjusted, if possible.

Cost-Effectiveness

It is possible to measure virtually anything. However, the results achieved from some measurement activities are simply not worth the investment necessary to collect and/or analyze the data. Therefore, when proposing performance measurement initiatives, leaders must determine the ultimate value of the measurement project

Table 1-4. Examples of Common and Special Cause Variation in Ambulatory Health Care Settings

Type of Variation	Example
Common Cause	1. Varying levels of patient acuity 2. Overall progress made by patients toward achievement of specified treatment goals 3. Number of patients seen daily 4. Percentage of incomplete patient records
Special Cause	1. Increased volume of patients seeking laser surgery for varicose veins following an extensive multimedia promotional campaign 2. Increase in telephone calls from parents to independent practitioners following frequent news stories about several cases of bacterial meningitis in local children 3. Damage to client records because of burst water pipes in the record room 4. Increased use of prison health services because of an outbreak of food poisoning

and the data it will generate. Acquiring valid, reliable, usable data that yields meaningful information is essential. However, preserving some resources for testing and achieving improvements is equally essential. Every measurement initiative requires a judgment-based decision: Will the magnitude of the expected improvement be worth the cost of the measurement?

Planning and Promoting Effective Outcomes Measurement

To help focus outcomes measurement and increase the likelihood of its benefit, consider answers to the following six questions:

1. What is the focus of outcomes measurement?
2. Does the selection of the outcomes measure(s) make sense?
3. Are the outcomes measures reliable?
4. Are the outcomes measures valid in the specific applications for which they will be used?
5. Are the outcomes measures sufficiently responsive to change?
6. Does the burden of using the outcomes measures exceed available resources?[5]

EXERCISE BREAK

Take a few moments to complete Worksheet #2: Reviewing The Effectiveness Of Performance Measurement, which is on pages 133–136 in the Appendix. Part I is a grid to help you assess the effectiveness of the measurement initiatives within your ambulatory care organization. Parts II and III offer a structure for developing a plan to address ineffective measurement efforts.

Benefits of Outcomes Measurement

Contemporary management of ambulatory care organizations is an outcomes-focused, data-driven discipline. The proactive management of outcomes requires the assessment, improvement, and control of performance through the collection and analysis of both process and outcomes data. This is the new strategic imperative. Although outcomes measurement is not a remedy, organizations can realize genuine benefits by conducting it.

Helps Improve Outcomes/Improve Processes

An organization that is outcomes oriented and process minded can improve in both areas. Processes can be altered in a systematic fashion in order to facilitate the accomplishment of desired outcomes. Processes can also be modified to enhance their operational effectiveness or efficiency. In either case, outcomes measurement is the vehicle for improving the way work is done (the process) and the organization performance level (the outcome). Such improvement in processes and outcomes applies to care processes and clinical outcomes, as well as administrative and business processes and operational and financial outcomes.

Fosters a Climate of Self-Evaluation

Outcomes measurement demonstrates an organization's commitment to objective analysis and systematic performance improvement. Once this value for self-assessment takes root within an ambulatory care organization, ongoing critical performance evaluation will flourish.

Supports Organization Viability

The survival of health care delivery organizations requires astute clinical and business judgment based on facts. Organization survival and prosperity in an increasingly competitive marketplace requires the collection and analysis of outcomes data, the comparison of organization performance to normative national standards, and improvement in the quality of care provided.[6]

Responds to Purchaser Demand

Purchasers of health care benefits are rapidly becoming educated about the processes and outcomes of clinical care. Cost containment is a high priority when selecting health care benefits. Yet purchasers are also seeking value.[7] Outcomes measurement is a powerful, although underutilized, tool for expressing the relationship between achieved results and the resources consumed to achieve those results. Table 1-5, page 10, provides a summary of the benefits of outcomes measurement.

THOUGHT BREAK

■ *Consider the benefits of performance measurement and determine which of these your ambulatory care organization has realized.*

■ *Identify any other benefits that have occurred because of effective measurement.*

■ *Review how these positive effects have been communicated to various interested audiences.*

Key Points

1. The relationship between processes and outcomes is the critical focal point for performance improvement.

2. The organization performance improvement process is reminiscent of the clinical care process.

3. There are three kinds of performance measures: structure, process, and outcomes.

4. The same or similar measures may be used to achieve the major purposes of performance measurement: assessment, improvement, and control.

5. Performance improvement results from measuring, assessing, and managing variation in processes and outcomes.

6. Effective measurement is relevant, comprehensive, cost-effective, and manageable. It employs reliable and valid measures and measurement instruments. It exposes the type and magnitude of variation.

7. Outcomes measurement has multiple benefits, including improved organization performance, enhanced ability to respond to stakeholder demands, and strengthened organization viability.

References

1. Schraeder C, et al: Population-based research data as a means to address health outcomes. *Journal of Ambulatory Care Management* pp 39–46, Oct 1997.

2. Joint Commission on Accreditation of Healthcare Organizations: *The Measurement Mandate.* Oakbrook Terrace, IL, 1993.

Table 1-5. Benefits of Effective Outcomes Measurement

1. Provides factual evidence of performance

2. Promotes ongoing organization self-evaluation and improvement

3. Illustrates improvement

4. Facilitates cost/benefit analyses

5. Helps to meet external requirements/demands for performance evaluation

6. May facilitate the establishment of long-term relationships with various external stakeholders

7. May differentiate organization from competitors

8. May contribute to the receipt of business contracts

9. Fosters organization survival

---

3. O'Leary MR: *Clinical Performance Data: A Guide to Interpretation.* Oakbrook Terrace, IL, 1996.

4. Lawthers J, Wood P: In search of psychiatric performance measures. *Clinical Performance and Quality Health Care* 4(1):38–40, Jan–Feb 1996.

5. Radosevich DM: A framework for selecting outcome measures for ambulatory care research. *Journal of Ambulatory Care Management* 20(4):1–9, Oct 1997.

6. Rosenblum B, Johann J, Bulich R: Designing your outcomes program and demonstrating the results. *Infusion* pp 34–38, May 1996.

7. Davies AR, et al: Outcomes assessment in clinical settings: A consensus statement on principles and best practices in project management. *Jt Comm J Qual Improv* 20:6–16, Jan 1994.

Chapter 2:

Committing to Organizationwide Performance Improvement

This chapter does the following:

1. Differentiates the performance improvement process from performance improvement projects;

2. Identifies cultural success factors that are essential for organizationwide performance improvement;

3. Provides guidance on selecting a performance improvement methodology for consistent use across the organization;

4. Suggests ways to identify and prioritize organization improvement opportunities; and

5. Describes an approach for maximizing organization capability for performance measurement and improvement.

The Performance Improvement Process Versus a Performance Improvement Project

Performance improvement can be most accurately conceptualized as a philosophy. This philosophy can be translated into defined action steps that foster continuous organization learning and improvement through self-evaluation and planned experimentation.

Ambulatory care organizations committed to ongoing outcomes improvement as a part of daily work examine the

■ effectiveness and efficiency of their defined core processes, such as access, scheduling, registration/admission, assessment and reassessment, treatment planning (initial and revisions), provision of interventions, follow-up, consultation, referral, documentation, and billing;

■ efficacy of treatments for specific patient populations, such as children with congenital cleft palate, college students with sexually transmitted diseases, adults suffering from chronic pain syndromes, and seniors with cataracts;

■ effectiveness and continuity of different ambulatory care services, such as antenatal care, treatment for physical abuse, physical therapy, diagnostic imaging, and sleep studies; and

■ appropriateness of different interventions, such as patient education, biofeedback for headache management, therapeutic endoscopy, tooth extraction, laser treatment for varicose veins, and skin grafting.

Ambulatory care organizations that successfully improve their own performance are typically engaged in multiple improvement projects simultaneously. Although the individual projects may differ, the approach used for improvement is consistent across the improvement projects and throughout the organization.

Fundamentally, an organization's *performance improvement process* is a carefully chosen, strategically driven, values-based, systematic, organizationwide approach to the achievement of specific, meaningful, high-priority organization improvements. *Performance improvement projects* are the diverse, individual, focused initiatives in which an organization invests in order to achieve clearly defined, important, and measurable performance improvements.

THOUGHT BREAK

■ *Think about performance improvement at your organization.*

■ *What is your organization's philosophy regarding quality?*

■ *How is the importance of continuous improvement expressed in your facility?*

■ *Do staff and management understand performance improvement in the same way? If not, how are the understandings different?*

■ *Can you define, describe, and differentiate the performance improvement process and projects at your organization?*

■ *What is your "gut impression" on how successful quality improvement has been in your organization?*

Establishing the Culture for Success

Leadership Commitment

Professional literature emphasizes the importance a leader plays in creating an organization that demands and supports continuous improvement. Although individual leadership styles may vary, the need for an organization's leaders to "lead for improvement" remains unchanged. What does this mean for the administrative and clinical leaders in ambulatory care organizations? What does it mean for the staff of such organizations? And most importantly, what does it mean for the patients?

Because an ambulatory care organization is dynamic, any movement or shift in one area affects all other areas. Leaders affect how staff work, which in turn affects how patients experience the service or product the organization delivers. Thus, the role of leadership is so important. Who leaders are and how they function in the organization directly affects the work of the organization's staff (process operations) and indirectly affects the experiences of the organization's patients (outcomes achieved).

What should leaders do to facilitate continuous improvement in organization performance? Contemporary organization leaders are challenged to embrace a new work, according to Peter M. Senge, director of the Systems Thinking and Organizational Learning Program at the Massachusetts Institute of Technology, Sloan School of Management. This new work is the building of learning organizations, which consciously and actively use all daily work activities as opportunities to learn and expand knowledge. When studied, these opportunities yield new information that can be used to improve performance. Senge summarizes the essential work of leaders:[1]

> Leadership in learning organizations centers on subtler and ultimately more important work. In a learning organization, leaders' roles differ dramatically from that of the charismatic decision-maker. Leaders are designers, teachers, and stewards. These roles require new skills: the ability to build shared vision, to bring to the surface and challenge prevailing mental models, and to foster more systemic patterns of thinking. In short, leaders in learning organizations are responsible for building organizations where people are continually expanding their capabilities to shape their future—that is, leaders are responsible for learning.

The concept of principle-centered leadership was promulgated by Stephen R. Covey, founder and chairman of the Covey Leadership Center and the Institute for Principle-Centered Leadership in Provo, Utah. Principle-centered leadership represents a paradigm shift away from traditional management philosophies to a more humanistic and spiritually-focused viewpoint. This new paradigm is anchored in a leader's deep understanding of humanity.

Table 2-1. Stephen Covey's Characteristics of Principle-Centered Leaders[2]

Characteristic	Description
Continually learning	All experiences are used for self-education. Continually seeking to expand knowledge, skills, and competence.
Service-oriented	View life as a mission and self as a steward. Committed to responsibility, service, and contribution.
Radiate positive energy	Have cheerful, pleasant, and happy countenances; positive, upbeat, and optimistic attitudes; enthusiastic, hopeful, believing spirits.
Believe in other people	Believe in the unseen potential of other people. Are compassionate and forgiving. Refuse to label, stereotype, categorize, or prejudge people. Create a climate for growth and opportunity for all.
Lead balanced lives	Have integrated all elements of themselves: personality, values and beliefs, feelings, thoughts, behaviors and actions. Have a solid self-esteem. Are rational and discerning, balanced, temperate, moderate, and wise. Are direct and forthright, not manipulative. Aware of and responsible for own strengths and weaknesses.
View life as an adventure	Are self-secure, flexible, and able to embrace experiences as "here and now" opportunities for new awareness, learning, and growth. Demonstrate initiative, resourcefulness, creativity, willpower, courage, stamina, and native intelligence.
Are synergistic	Are change agents who are productive in new and creative ways. Optimize the strengths and capabilities and minimize the weaknesses of all. Are able to build coherent, cohesive, successful teams. Are able to negotiate win/win solutions.
Exercise for self-renewal	Make time to respond to own personal physical, mental, emotional, and spiritual needs.

Principle-centered leaders are fair, kind, efficient, effective, and wholistic. They understand people as spiritual beings searching for meaning, a sense of purpose, and a feeling of contribution. Dr. Covey has identified eight key traits that characterize leaders who are principle-centered.[2] Table 2-1, above, presents a brief description of these characteristics.

Patricia McLagan and Christo Nel, co-directors of the Democracy and Work Institute in South Africa, emphasize that transformative leadership is required if an organization is to live an authentic, observable commitment to total quality improvement. This new role of leaders requires them to guide organizations from compartmentalization and authoritarianism to participative involvement and interdependence. Table 2-2, page 14, offers a step-by-step guide to help leaders personify this new leadership style.[3]

Executive leadership plays a crucial role in creating an organization that measures, assesses, and continuously improves performance. Leadership by senior management is the most critical success factor for organization performance improvement;[4] Table 2-3, page 15, provides

---

Table 2-2. Step-by-Step Guide to the New Style of Leadership[3]

1. Acknowledge the need for and commit to personal change. Then, look deep within and transform oneself.

2. Create direct, respectful, meaningful relationships with employees at all levels.

3. Direct and lead organization change. Help managers and direct service staff to change and develop the capacity to function effectively in an empowered environment. Be prepared to deal proactively and productively with the fear, insecurity, self doubt, confusion, frustration, and hostility such change is likely to evoke.

4. Create and sustain a vision of the future organization. Ensure that all staff understand the vision and how their efforts support its achievement.

5. Build investment in and strength throughout the organization by sharing information widely with staff. Create an open environment with a climate that nurtures the development of personal leadership, creativity, responsibility, and capability in staff at all levels in the organization.

6. Reframe the definition of leadership so that all staff are expected to demonstrate the initiative and effort essential to continuous performance improvement.

---

a list of specific actions that leaders can take to advance the evolution of continuous performance improvement within their organization.

THOUGHT BREAK

■ *Consider your own perspective on leadership in organizations.*

■ *What do you believe to be the most important characteristics of effective leaders?*

■ *What leaders have you admired?*

■ *Why did you admire them?*

■ *How do you demonstrate leadership in your daily work?*

■ *Given the opportunity, what would be the single most important recommendation you would offer the top leaders in your organization about how they could become more effective in their leadership roles?*

Build Staff Understanding and Participation

Leadership is necessary, but not sufficient, for organization performance improvement. By

themselves, leaders simply cannot improve organization performance. Therefore, effective leadership for improvement both expects and demands employee involvement. Each employee is responsible for an organization's performance and for the improvement of its performance. Properly supportive leadership maximizes the organization's total capacity for improvement. Staff must take the following steps to make meaningful contributions to organization performance improvement:

■ Understand the mission, vision, and values of the organization;

■ Recognize the contribution of their work to the fulfillment of the mission and accomplishment of the vision;

■ Understand the value of continuous organization improvement, from both the organization's and patients' perspectives;

■ Recognize their own critical role in improving organization performance;

■ Become familiar with the principles of continuous improvement;

■ Learn about the tools and techniques of performance improvement;

■ Become adept at measuring, assessing, and improving the performance of their own work processes and outcomes;

Table 2-3. Leadership Actions that Advance the Evolution of Continuous Improvement of Organization Performance

1. Communicate the importance and value of continuous improvement of organization performance.

2. Define the executive leadership as the formal oversight body responsible for ongoing improvement of organization performance.

3. Require that a performance improvement plan, which supports the achievement of strategic goals and objectives, is drafted, implemented, and routinely monitored.

4. Ensure that the organization adopts, adapts, or develops one single, consistent approach or method for systematic improvement.

5. Become educated in the principles and practices of performance improvement and performance measurement.

6. Role model the use of performance measurement and improvement tools and data-based leadership, decision making, and improvement.

7. Manage by asking questions that require the collection, interpretation, and use of performance data.

8. Allocate the resources, including education and personnel, necessary for improvement.

9. Include specific competencies for organization performance improvement in job descriptions and performance appraisals for all staff.

10. Avoid using performance data, performance measurement, and performance improvement projects for disciplinary or punitive purposes.

- Receive both public and private recognition for their improvement efforts; and
- Strive always to solicit and understand patients' needs and experiences of the organization.

THOUGHT BREAK

- *Think about your job and role responsibilities.*

- *How does what you do everyday support the achievement of your organization's mission?*

- *In what ways are you contributing to the accomplishment of the future vision of your organization?*

- *Are you routinely making improvements in your own work processes and outcomes?*

- *Have you determined who your immediate customers are?*

- *Do you know what they need from you?*

- *Are you familiar with improvement tools? If yes, do you use them in your work? If no, how can you learn about them and apply them in your work?*

- *What is the single most important recommendation you would give to yourself about how you could become more effective in your role?*

Establish Partnerships with Stakeholders

Many individuals and groups are interested in understanding the processes and outcomes of ambulatory care organizations. Patients want contemporary services provided in a professional, competent, and caring manner. Purchasers want affordable, state-of-the-art services targeted to the needs of their beneficiaries. Payers seek value—the least costly care that can be provided safely. Other stakeholders, such as accrediting bodies and regulatory agencies, look for the ethical provision of effective and appropriate care that results in positive patient outcomes.

Ambulatory care organizations must interact effectively with all these stakeholders, despite their often conflicting agendas. Building partnerships with such vested parties is no small task; doing so requires diligence, patience, political acumen, and outstanding interpersonal skills to forge a mutual understanding of each other's interests. Ambulatory care organizations must agree with all stakeholders. This agreement must promise that the most appropriate care will be provided at the least possible cost.

Once this consensus occurs, the ambulatory care facility must direct its attention to understanding the specific and unique performance data/information needs of each stakeholder. This can be accomplished by asking a series of focused questions. Once the data/information needs are known, constructing a meaningful performance report becomes possible. Such a report should be designed with brevity, clarity, and completeness in mind. The stakeholders should know the meaning and implications of the data/information in the performance report. The pertinence and usefulness of the report should be evaluated. Then, the report should be revised until it presents the required data/information in the most easy-to-understand format.

Selection and Use of a Performance Improvement Methodology

To facilitate a planned, organized, and consistent approach to improvement, organization leaders should select and require the use of one improvement method for all performance improvement initiatives. Potential sources of improvement methodologies include

- the Joint Commission's cycle for improving performance, as described in the

EXERCISE BREAK

Take a few moments to complete Worksheet #3: Assessment of Stakeholder's Data/Information Needs, which is on pages 137–139 in the Appendix. Part I asks you to list your organization's stakeholders who have data or information needs. Part II is an interview guide that can be used to clarify and specify the data and information needs and uses of each stakeholder. You may also find the completion of this worksheet to be a useful component of a performance measurement effort.

"Improving Organization Performance" chapter of the *Comprehensive Accreditation Manual for Ambulatory Care* (*CAMAC*);

- books and journal articles addressing strategies for improving the performance of health care delivery organizations;
- consulting firms that develop, test, refine, and use a proprietary and/or copyrighted improvement methodology (such as Ernst and Young's IMPROVE method); and
- health care systems and organizations that have developed and successfully used a performance improvement method (such as FOCUS-PDCA [Plan-Do-Check-Act], which was developed at the Hospital Corporation of America).

An ambulatory care organization may elect to develop its own performance improvement method, one that is custom-designed for that organization's unique environment and specific to the patient population being served.

Many individual improvement methods have been developed. Their specific steps and the language used may vary. However, few significant differences exist among these methods. In fact, all are anchored in the scientific method, which asks the following questions:

1. What is currently known about the issue of interest?
2. What else about this issue needs to be known?
3. What changes are proposed?
4. What is the anticipated impact of these changes?

Table 2-4. Performance Improvement Method Selection Criteria

1. Consistency with the organization's stated mission, vision, and performance improvement philosophy;

2. Logical and easy to understand;

3. Easy to implement and use; and

4. Specifies clear, distinct action steps that include

   a. issue identification,

   b. identification of improvement goals,

   c. measurement and assessment of current performance,

   d. analysis of root causes of performance,

   e. generation and prioritization of improvement actions,

   f. pilot testing of proposed improvement actions, and

   g. institutionalization of proven improvement actions.

5. How can these proposed changes be tested?
6. What occurred as a result of testing these changes?
7. Which tested changes should be adopted?

Leaders must remember that an improvement method provides a structure for learning about current performance and identifying and testing changes that can improve future performance. The Joint Commission has addressed performance improvement methods in detail in other publications. Interested readers are referred to *Framework For Improving Performance, Cycle For Improving Performance: A Pocket Guide, Performance Improvement In Ambulatory Care,* and *Using Performance Improvement Tools In Ambulatory Care.*

Selection Criteria

The decision to use one particular performance improvement method should be based on clearly defined, reasonable selection criteria. Table 2-4, above, offers a list of such selection criteria that can be used when choosing a performance improvement method.

Using the Chosen Improvement Methodology

Once your organization's leaders have selected an improvement method, they should require its use in all improvement activities. To facilitate this, leaders must communicate to all staff that an improvement method has been chosen and from then on will be used consistently across the organization *without exception*. At this juncture, providing a written explanation of the improvement method, its advantages, and why it was selected for use is often helpful.

Your organization's leaders should offer detailed education about how to make the improvement method operational, as well as how to actually proceed through its defined steps, in a just-in-time fashion. Learning how to use the method to achieve actual performance improvement should occur at the initiation and throughout each improvement project. Individuals are then able to apply their new knowledge and skills in a real and meaningful work activity.

Staff will inevitably look for short cuts, or ways to complete tasks more quickly. Indeed, the search for efficiencies is a critical component of all performance improvement processes. However, to maintain the integrity of the improvement method, each step must be completed sequentially and no steps should be skipped. This may appear to be rigid adherence to an arbitrary set of rules. In actuality, it affords the structure and discipline necessary to design creative solutions.

Leaders must evaluate continuously how well the chosen performance improvement method works. As each improvement team completes its charge, it should critique the improvement method as a part of its overall assessment of the improvement process. Did the method in fact meet all the selection criteria against which it was originally assessed? Specifically, what components of the method worked well, enabling effective and efficient work? What aspects of the method failed to work well or disabled productive work? Anecdotal stories about the improvement method should be solicited and analyzed for dominant themes and trends. This content analysis should then be shared with top management. Ultimately, as a part of their performance improvement oversight responsibilities, leaders must decide whether to continue to use the chosen method or select a new and alternative improvement methodology.

THOUGHT BREAK

- *Think about how performance improvements are made in your organization.*

- *What improvement method is used?*

- *How was this method chosen?*

- *How did you learn about this organization approach to performance improvement?*

- *Is the chosen method used systematically and consistently? If not, why not?*

- *How is the improvement methodology evaluated?*

- *Has it ever been revised based on evaluative feedback?*

- *What should be done to help all staff within your organization understand this improvement method?*

Determining Areas for Improvement

Numerous opportunities for improvement exist in every ambulatory care organization. However, not all improvements are of the same magnitude. Improvements that are powerful and worthy of organization resources include those that will positively impact a large number of patients; eliminate or reduce instability in critical clinical or business processes; decrease patient, staff, or organization risk; ameliorate serious problems; and optimize the likelihood of consistently achieving desired clinical and business outcomes.

Leaders are responsible for determining what improvement efforts will produce the greatest gain for the organization. The decisions to allocate improvement resources must support the organization's mission, vision, and strategic clinical and business priorities. In working to identify a complementary mix of performance improvement priorities, leaders must consider their organization's strategic plan, performance improvement plan, operational plans and budgets, as well as contemporary clinical and business practices. When selecting improvement initiatives, leaders must also weigh the changing needs of consumers of services and other stakeholders' requirements.

In striving to specify improvement priorities, leaders must also consider what available performance data reveals about process operations and achieved outcomes. Not every measured process and outcome will become an improvement priority. Performance in many measured areas will be deemed to be acceptable. In such cases, an appropriate goal may be to simply sustain current performance. In some instances, performance may not achieve desirable levels, but because of relatively low impact or the potential for only small gains, such areas may also not be targeted for improvement. Only those areas that significantly affect important clinical processes, critical clinical outcomes, key business results, the organization's core functions, and the primary needs of patients should be considered as priorities for improvement.

Leaders should also seek staff input when determining high priority improvements. Staff, especially direct service and support staff, often have a highly focused and correct perception of patients' needs and wants. In addition, staff typically have an accurate understanding, based on empirical knowledge, of the flaws, inconsistencies, and vulnerabilities of important clinical and nonclinical processes. They are usually able to accurately forecast the resources and timelines necessary to achieve and sustain improvement. This is one of the most compelling reasons for engaging staff in performance improvement activities.

Once improvement priorities are determined, rank them in order from most to least urgent. The executive leadership then must develop a performance improvement agenda that realistically reflects the organization's true capacity for improvement, given all the other daily work and special projects that are in process. At this point, leaders should communicate widely to staff throughout the ambulatory care organization about the chosen improvement priorities. Explanations of why the specific projects were selected, enthusiastic expression of the value of these projects, and public support for and acknowledgment of the projects should be voiced. Leaders must allocate the necessary resources so that the high priority improvement projects can begin.

Building Organization Capability for Performance Measurement and Improvement

The knowledge and skills for performance measurement and improvement are not innate or pervasive in contemporary organizations. What is present, and must be unleashed, is the potential for improvement and innovation. Leaders should nurture the organization's capability to improve. Building organization capacity for performance improvement involves several very visible and concrete leadership actions, which are summarized in Table 2-5, page 21.

EXERCISE BREAK

Take a few moments to complete Worksheet #4: Determining Areas For Organization Improvement, which is on pages 140–143 in the Appendix. This worksheet will guide you through a series of focusing questions to help you determine your organization's current performance improvement priorities. You may also find the completion of this worksheet to be a useful component of your organization strategic and quality planning processes.

Establish a Performance Improvement Oversight Body

A group with decision-making authority should be convened and invested with the responsibility of overseeing all aspects of the organization's performance improvement process. In a highly subspecialized or small ambulatory organization, such a group may include two or three individuals. For instance, a physician director may simultaneously represent both clinical and administrative issues, while a nurse offers guidance in structuring and conducting improvement initiatives. In more resource-rich ambulatory care organizations, this oversight group may include clinical and administrative leaders, performance improvement resource staff, human relations/staff development personnel, marketing or public relations staff, and one or more staff representatives. The skeleton of this group is often found in the organization's senior management group. Usually, the proper group composition is achieved by adding one or two additional individuals.

The Performance Improvement Oversight Body is fundamentally responsible for

- determining improvement priorities;
- integrating performance improvement into daily work;
- initiating performance improvement projects;
- monitoring the progress of improvement efforts;
- acting on recommendations for specific improvement actions/changes; and

HIGH RISK, HIGH VOLUME, PROBLEM-PRONE

When confronted with a virtually endless array of measurement opportunities, determining what to measure is a challenging and often confusing experience. The Joint Commission's recommendation, first made more than ten years ago, to examine high risk, high volume, and problem prone areas is still useful advice today.

As you think about how to allocate your organization's performance measurement resources, consider those populations you serve that are particularly vulnerable, fragile, or unstable. Review the risks involved in providing care and service to such a group of patients. Identify the possible outcomes of failing to provide the right treatment in the right way. Think also of those care practices that are investigational, new, or particularly risky. Then build measures that will facilitate the collection of performance data in such high risk areas.

Review the case mix of patients your organization serves. Identify the demographic characteristics of your population of patients. Determine if your treatment services are targeted at a particular age group or diagnostic category. Consider whether your organization offers a specific treatment approach or intervention for a variety of patients with differing needs. Then, identify performance measures that will capture data that reveals how well your organization is performing in such high volume areas.

Finally, examine the etiology and distribution of the most compelling problems that confront your organization. Look for particular areas where processes seem to break down. Identify those areas in which it is very difficult to achieve desired outcomes or implement procedures consistently. Look for trends and patterns of problems. Then adopt, adapt, or create measures that will acquire data, perhaps as an "early warning system," that will describe performance in such problem-prone areas.

The Dimensions of Performance

The Joint Commission has identified the following nine dimensions of performance: efficacy, appropriateness, availability, timeliness, effectiveness, continuity, safety, efficiency, and respect and caring.

As you strive to define what to measure, consider how each of these performance dimensions relates to the different populations of patients your organization serves and the various important clinical and non-clinical functions that operate within your organization. Create measures based on the intersection of dimension, patient population, and function. For instance, meaningful measures may include

1. therapeutic effects and side effects of oral steroids prescribed for individuals with chronic obstructive pulmonary disease (COPD) (examines the effectiveness [dimension] of pharmacotherapy [clinical function] in individuals with COPD [patient population]);
2. frequency of well-baby screenings at the local health department (examines the availability [dimension] of assessment of patients [clinical function] in infants and babies [patient population]); and
3. scheduling of prenatal care visits at the Indian Health Center (examines the timeliness [dimension] of patient care [clinical function] in pregnant Native American women [patient population]).

■ communicating improvements within and outside the organization.

In the interest of resource conservation, especially in organizations with a small staff, these responsibilities can be effectively and efficiently integrated into the usual and customary leadership activities of clinicians and administrators. In turn, this can result in an ambulatory care organization using performance improvement processes as the way it conducts its daily work.

Table 2-5. Leadership Actions Necessary for Building Organization Capacity for Improvement

1. Establish a performance improvement oversight body.

2. Define a mechanism to coordinate performance improvement initiatives.

3. Develop performance improvement protocols.

4. Identify and respond to performance improvement resource needs.

5. Recognize and acknowledge performance improvement successes and efforts.

6. Continuously assess the effectiveness of the organization's improvement efforts.

Define a Mechanism to Coordinate Performance Improvement Initiatives

The quality oversight group typically delegates the day-to-day coordination and support of performance improvement projects. In resource-rich organizations, staff may be dedicated solely to performance improvement. Often, however, responsibilities for performance improvement are coupled with multiple other patient care and management functions. In either case, the staff that support performance improvement typically

- help to initiate improvement projects;
- provide just-in-time performance improvement education;
- quantify resource consumption for each improvement project;
- track and record the progress of each improvement project; and
- develop performance improvement protocols.

Develop Performance Improvement Protocols

Performance improvement protocols basically describe how a particular organization makes its performance improvement process and methodology operational. The protocols themselves are usually drafted by performance improvement professionals or other staff knowledgeable in performance improvement processes and techniques. However, they are always reviewed and approved by the performance improvement

oversight body and the organization's executive management (if they are not included in the oversight body).

Performance improvement protocols typically describe the

- purpose and responsibilities of the performance improvement oversight body;
- process for proposing improvement projects;
- process for reviewing and selecting improvement projects;
- way(s) to create and convene performance improvement project teams;
- role responsibilities of various improvement team members, including the leader, members, facilitator, and executive coach or champion;
- organization's chosen performance improvement method and how to operationalize it;
- performance improvement project documentation requirements;
- reporting/communication requirements for performance improvement projects; and
- ways that successful performance improvement is acknowledged, recognized, and rewarded.

These protocols need not be complicated, nor is sophisticated documentation required. Often, such protocols can be readily integrated into existing strategic plans, human resource plans and guidelines, policies, and/or procedures.

Doing so helps to link quality functions to the daily work of providing care and service to patients.

Identify and Respond to Performance Improvement Resource Needs

Organization performance improvement must be cultivated. This requires investment and support as well as concrete resources such as expert help, time, information and knowledge, equipment, and money. Finding and allocating these resources in an organization with significant economic and time constraints requires creativity and a willingness to test untried approaches to resource acquisition and deployment. Organization leaders who are committed to successful performance improvement must be prepared to respond to five kinds of resource needs:

1. An organization must have ready access to a performance improvement *resource person.* This individual provides consultation, coaching, and education to improvement teams, management, and staff. Although it is not required, many ambulatory care organizations have a designated resource person on staff. In small organizations, this individual usually carries multiple professional responsibilities. Some organizations are able to dedicate one or more full-time staff to performance improvement functions.

    Many community colleges and universities have or are developing curricula that focus on total quality management. Students in such programs often look for "internships"—opportunities to apply their new knowledge and practice newly learned skills. Establishing partnerships with such academic institutions can help to fill a resource void within your organization.

    Participation in national or regional "health care quality demonstration projects" often affords an organization the opportunity to consult with performance improvement/measurement experts. Organization involvement in such projects can yield multiple benefits including access to experienced professionals who can offer both formal and informal education and recommendations

about selecting and implementing performance improvement initiatives within your organization.

2. Employees need *time* to work on performance improvement teams and projects. Top management, middle management, and staff must agree that employee participation in performance improvement initiatives is a high-priority job responsibility. Involvement in performance improvement activities should be included in the accountabilities of all position descriptions and as a performance factor addressed during annual performance appraisals. Managers and staff must work together creatively to ensure that employee involvement in performance improvement activities occurs routinely, but does not cause unnecessary disruptions in other work processes.

    Because planning for performance improvement initiatives requires focused attention, analysis, and decision making, it generally occurs as a discrete activity. Once appropriately planned, however, the application of improvement processes and techniques and the implementation of performance improvement projects can and should be made a part of everyday work.

    For instance, while seeing patients or documenting the patient encounter, clinicians can easily complete brief data collection instruments in the patient's medical record. Key operational outcomes, such as missed and rescheduled appointments, can be documented and monitored each day by reception staff as they are notified by patients and practitioners of changes. Perhaps numbers of patients seen by practitioner can be tallied on a check sheet by the assistant who escorts the patient to the examining room. Accounting staff can manually or electronically log billing time and numbers of invoices sent at the time the billing statements are generated.

    Basic quality improvement tools can be used throughout the course of the work week to examine and improve nagging problems. For example, clerical staff can create a process flow diagram that defines how abnormal laboratory results are managed. After identifying how they receive test results and communicating them to practitioners, support staff can post this beginning flow chart on the wall of a commonly used staff area. During a few free moments, clinicians providing direct patient care can informally document how they address the abnormal lab results with their patients. Support staff can then transcribe the completed flow chart into a neat, legible document showing all the different, and often conflicting, process steps. This "master" flow chart would be distributed to all involved staff with instructions to review it, generate improvement ideas, write their suggestions directly on the flow chart, and return it to the coordinating clerical staff. Once again, support staff would transcribe the input into a comprehensive list of possible improvements to be addressed at a regular staff meeting. During the meeting, staff can identify the most promising recommended improvements, choose which to test, develop a reasonable test plan, and create a brief process performance assessment tool that can be used to collect data on the operations and results of the tested process improvements. These performance data can be reviewed at a future staff meeting and used to make data-based decisions about which improvements will be a routine part of the process for handling abnormal lab results.

Such "institutionalization" of systematic performance improvement approaches is beneficial to all organizations. However, it is especially helpful for those organizations that cannot dedicate time to extra, additional, or special improvement projects. In fact, doing the daily work of caring for patients or supporting the care of patients by using systematic performance improvement processes may be the *only way* small ambulatory care organizations or those with limited resources can realistically and successfully improve their performance.

3. Individuals and teams must learn how to improve organization performance. Therefore, resources for *education* about the

principles of continuous improvement, the basic and advanced quality improvement tools, performance measurement, performance assessment, and the organization's selected improvement methodology must be readily available to staff and teams as they initiate and carry out their assigned performance improvement projects. Generic, didactic performance improvement training has not been demonstrated to be helpful. What is helpful and needed is focused education aimed at enabling staff to successfully take the next step in a specific, current improvement project.

Building true *organization* knowledge for improvement demands a planned and methodical strategy aimed at optimizing existing strengths and available resources. Ambulatory care organizations of all types, structures, and sizes must identify realistic ways of enhancing staff capability for performance improvement. Only then can the organization's genuine capacity for improvement be maximized. There are many relatively inexpensive ways to infuse an ambulatory care organization with performance improvement information and knowledge. Some suggestions follow:

a. National/local membership and active participation in key professional organizations, such as the National Association for Healthcare Quality (NAHQ) or the American Society for Quality (ASQ), create an accessible performance improvement resource network of people, projects, journals, books, and so forth. Association memberships commonly result in learning partnerships among individuals and organizations. These relationships provide opportunity for "no cost" consultation, cost-free or low-cost exchange of staff development offerings at the different partner organizations, cross-organization work and interest groups, process benchmarking, and the like.

b. Subscribing to key journals, such as *The Joint Commission Journal on Quality Improvement, Journal for Healthcare Quality, Total Quality Management Review, Quality Digest, Journal for Quality and Participation,*

Sloan Management Review, Quality Progress, and so on, brings current quality concepts and cutting edge ideas about performance improvement directly into your ambulatory care organization. Facilitating a "quality journal club" during regularly scheduled staff meetings is an effective way to actively engage staff in performance improvement-focused dialogue and learning.

c. Membership and participation in local business consortia affords the opportunity to network with, learn from, and establish relationships with high performing industries from surrounding communities. Much can be learned from both manufacturing and service businesses that have successfully implemented total quality management and/or continuous quality improvement. Typically, these organizations can demonstrate how to achieve substantial cost savings through the application of quality processes.

d. Participation in local, state, national, and international quality awards creates an access route to many varied resources. Volunteer award application reviewers and examiners generally receive substantial education about the intent, meaning, and assessment of award criteria. Fundamentally, this instruction is learning about organization performance improvement. Typically, no fee is required for the training, although there may be transportation and lodging costs. Simply reviewing quality award application forms and considering your organization's performance in relation to the award application categories provides an intense learning experience. Completing the application, either as an internal self-assessment process or in an effort to win the award, will lead to a deep understanding of how your organization actually operates in the key areas (for example, results/outcomes, process management, human resources management, leadership, customer service, information management, and so on) of the organization's performance infrastructure.

e. As previously noted, health care organizations will traditionally designate one or two key individuals as quality resource(s). This is often feasible and can prove helpful. However, deciding *whom* to designate is critical because, by definition, these individuals will assume a formal or informal organization leadership function. Therefore, chosen staff should have a strategic view, a general understanding of organizations as interdependent systems, and a working knowledge of the major functions of the ambulatory care organization. The quality resource(s) must be willing and able to reconstruct their own work style to one that reflects performance improvement values and approaches. The quality resource(s) staff can only be successful if the ambulatory care organization invests in their initial and continued learning about improving the performance of health care delivery organizations and promotes the implementation of their quality functions within the organization.

4. Meaningful performance improvement involves collection and analysis of complex, both clinical and nonclinical, process and outcomes data. The design and use of data collection instruments, the employment of improvement tools, the application of descriptive and analytic statistics, and the assessment of performance are challenging data management issues that can be made less time-consuming and difficult by using software packages. It is difficult, although not impossible, for staff to measure, assess, and improve outcomes and processes without some technological support. These *technology* needs must be examined and addressed by all organizations that are serious about improving performance in today's environment.

Ambulatory care organizations with large technology budgets can purchase one or more of the many quality/performance improvement or statistical process/quality control software packages. The sophistication, statistical capabilities, and graphic features vary widely among the products. Some packages are very user-friendly, exploiting health care professionals' "intuitive" appreciation of variation in performance. Other systems are more complicated and require a deeper understanding of statistical theory and application.

Remember, however, that the purchase of specialty software for performance measurement and improvement is not an essential requirement for sound data analysis and interpretation. Often, available software can be adopted or adapted for performance data analysis and presentation. Ambulatory care organizations affiliated with academic or research institutions may have access to one of the commonly used comprehensive statistical packages. Such software can readily calculate basic descriptive statistics, correlations, and control charts. Many ambulatory care organizations, including those with limited resources, often employ one of the commonly available database programs. Once appropriate formulas have been inserted, these programs can calculate control charts, run charts, and descriptive statistics. Even the most basic graphics programs can be used to create pie charts, bar graphs, pareto charts, and other pictorial presentations of data.

Those ambulatory care organizations that cannot rely on technological support for performance data management can still confidently collect, analyze, display, and act upon performance data. By keeping data collection tools simple; tallying data counts; "hand drawing" run charts; using calculators to determine rates, averages, and control limits; and manually drawing simple data charts and graphs, organization performance can be accurately and thoroughly understood. Also, subsequent improvement actions can be effectively focused on critical performance areas.

5. Organizations must commit *financial* resources to the performance improvement effort. The cost of staff time is the greatest improvement-related expense. Costs for training materials, technological resources, general supplies, and other expenses become significant when compared to the costs of all performance improvement projects implemented in a single fiscal year.

Each ambulatory care organization must determine what it can reasonably invest in performance improvement. These costs should not be viewed solely as an expense-driven cost center. When making resource allocation decisions, consider how effective performance improvement can reduce normal operating expenses, prevent or minimize direct/indirect costs of performance failures and inconsistencies, and contribute to increased revenue from existing services and/or the generation of additional revenue from new services or "product lines."

THOUGHT BREAK

- *Think about formal performance improvement initiatives that have been launched in your organization.*

- *What types of resources were dedicated to these efforts?*

- *Were they adequate? If not, why not?*

- *What needs to be done to effectively integrate performance improvement into your organization's day-to-day work?*

Recognize and Acknowledge Performance Improvement Successes and Efforts

Because improvement projects are focused on important organization priorities, many staff will be interested in knowing about the progress and results of such projects. Involving staff helps to build open communication, organizationwide teamwork, supportiveness, and professional pride. Acknowledging improvement successes builds organization momentum for future successes, engenders a sense of meaningful contribution in individual employees, and bonds the organization in celebration. Private recognition of improvement successes rewards teams and individuals by respecting and appreciating their unique talents, skills, and perspectives. In turn, this fosters employee loyalty and dedication. When leaders recognize, appreciate, and acknowledge achieved improvements and genuine efforts, they create a win/win experience for the entire organization and its individual employees. If leaders fail to support improvement efforts, they risk loss of credibility and contribute to staff demoralization.

Continuously Assess the Effectiveness of the Organization's Improvement Efforts

Because organizations are not static, the functions within them, including the measurement, assessment, and improvement of performance, are also not static. Leaders must regularly examine the effectiveness and pertinence of an organization's improvement processes, method, and projects. Traditionally, organization improvement plans have been reviewed and revised annually. Performance improvement efforts can be evaluated when conducting environmental assessments, revising strategic objectives, analyzing and updating strategic and operational plans, and preparing budgets. Just as an ambulatory care organization must remain current in clinical practice and business administration, it must also understand and use the most contemporary performance improvement knowledge, skills, and tools. A planned schedule for evaluating the improvement functions will help to keep them current, meaningful, and focused on the future.

EXERCISE BREAK

Take a few moments to complete Worksheet #5: Assessing Organization Commitment to Performance Measurement and Improvement, which is on pages 144–146 in the Appendix. Completing this worksheet will help you determine the readiness of your organization's leadership and staff to seriously commit to performance measurement and improvement. You may wish to engage your quality oversight body in completing this worksheet as an evaluation exercise to determine your organization's readiness for meaningful performance improvement.

Key Points

1. An organization's performance improvement process reflects its values and describes a single, consistent approach for conducting performance improvement projects.

2. Performance measurement and improvement will only succeed in an organization culture of support, inquiry, dialogue, teamwork, participation, continuous learning, and calculated risk taking.

3. The selection of a performance improvement methodology should be a thoughtful, criteria-based process. The effectiveness and ease of use of the chosen improvement method should be routinely evaluated by both improvement team members and organization leaders.

4. Leaders must rank in order of importance the many organization improvement opportunities. They must then make priority-based decisions about which improvement initiatives to implement. Resources must be committed to support the accomplishment of the chosen improvement projects.

5. The organization's capability for performance measurement and improvement should be developed proactively. Leaders should assess the organization's current capacity for improvement, compare this capacity to strategic improvement goals and objectives, identify any gaps or needs, and institute strategies to remediate any identified deficiencies.

References

1. Senge P: The leader's new work: Building learning organizations. *Sloan Management Review* pp 7–23, Fall 1990.

2. Covey S: *Principle-Centered Leadership.* New York: Summit Books, 1991.

3. McLagan P, Nel C: A new leadership style for genuine total quality. *Journal For Quality And Participation* 19(3):14–16, Jun 1996.

4. Roland C, et al: Insights into improving organizational performance. *Quality Progress* 30(3):82–85, Mar 1997.

Chapter 3:

Performance Measures Applicable to Ambulatory Care Organizations

---

This chapter does the following:

1. Defines "performance measure";

2. Describes a variety of sources of performance measures;

3. Summarizes the Joint Commission's *National Library of Healthcare Indicators* (*NLHI*);

4. Reviews the types of performance measures that are pertinent to ambulatory care organizations;

5. Explores the various categories of measures necessary for designing and implementing a balanced measurement model; and

6. Reviews patient perception of care and services (satisfaction) measures as a useful source of performance information.

Performance Measures

A performance measure or indicator, as it is sometimes called, is a quantitative tool (for example, rate, ratio, index, percentage) that provides an indication of an organization's performance in relation to a specified process or outcome. Quite simply, a performance measure is a tool for generating performance data. These data may be clinical or nonclinical. Clinical performance data are unbiased representations of patient care processes or health outcomes.[1] Nonclinical performance data typically reflect the operation and outcomes of key operational and administrative processes.

THOUGHT BREAK

- *Consider performance measures that are currently in use in your organization.*

- *What kinds of clinically-focused data do they produce?*

- *Do these clinical data reveal information about achieved outcomes or process operations?*

- *What kinds of operational data are available?*

- *What administrative/financial data are available?*

- *Do the operational and administrative/financial measures assess processes or outcomes, or both?*

Sources of Performance Measures

There are multiple sources of performance measures. These include subject matter experts, professional literature, professional associations, ambulatory care organizations that define customized measures, health systems that develop indicators for use by their affiliated care delivery sites, and other authorities. Both

THE NATIONAL LIBRARY OF HEALTHCARE INDICATORS

In 1997, the Joint Commission published the *National Library of Healthcare Indicators™: Health Plan and Network Edition (NLHI)*. It is a comprehensive catalog of indicators deemed by content experts to have face validity.

NLHI is a practical tool that organizes available, credible measures in a way that facilitates their use by a variety of interested parties. NLHI's indicators are classified into four broad categories:

1. Priority clinical conditions arrayed against domains of performance;
2. Health status, as depicted by priority clinical conditions arrayed against domains of performance;

3. Satisfaction from the perspectives of consumers/enrollees, practitioners and purchasers; and
4. Administrative and financial aspects of organization performance.

Each indicator in NLHI has its own profile that defines the measure, describes its focus and rationale, details its characteristics (including risk adjustment and stratification, if any), portrays its applicability to various health care delivery settings including ambulatory care organizations, and delineates the degree to which the indicator has been formally tested.

---

public and private organizations with a vested interest in health care may develop and make available performance measures.

Examples of Performance Measures

Quality of care researchers suggest that two types of information are needed to understand and improve the quality of medical care. First, the health care services provided to patients must be understood. Examples of measures that generate such knowledge are

- rates of disease screening in a defined patient population;

- percentage of patients receiving appropriate follow-up of abnormal diagnostic test results; and

- percentage of patients receiving ongoing medical therapies that are appropriately monitored by their care provider.

Second, the internal and external factors that influence the organization's ability to provide care must be understood. Data-based responses to the following types of questions must be sought:

- What are the differences in the practice patterns of part-time and full-time care providers?

- How does organization size affect practice?

- What personal experiences result in clinicians' promoting continuous improvement of organization performance?

By eliciting these complementary data, an ambulatory care organization can begin to develop an accurate, factual understanding of its performance.[2]

Four types of data are integral to an outcomes management program.[3] *Descriptive data* characterize a patient population. When these data are not complemented by other process and outcomes data, they do not provide enough information to contribute significantly to results management. Typical elements of descriptive data include patient age, gender, number/frequency of visits, primary care provider, consultants, payer, and diagnosis.

Clinical data create a picture of the patient's health status. Physiologic clinical data include such elements as vital signs, results of diagnostic tests, and treatment responses. Cognitive capabilities, thought processes, and emotional states are examples of psychological data. Clinical data that are collected after a diagnostic or therapeutic intervention always reflect an intermediate or final outcome, such as symptom relief or improvement in health. Quality of life, functional status, and satisfaction measures all produce outcomes data.

Operational data are essential for administrative decision making and judgments about organization operations. Operational data may examine clinically-related functions such as accessibility and availability of care providers. Utilization, productivity, costs, numbers, patterns, and competencies of staff are examples of operational data that have an administrative focus.

Benchmarking data allow for one type of comparative analysis. Clinical and nonclinical outcomes are frequently benchmarked. Average numbers of patients seen per provider, reimbursement rates, and treatment outcomes (including complications) are typical of data that are used for comparison purposes.[3]

Clinically focused outcomes measures relevant to ambulatory care settings examine dimensions of patient health in three key domains: clinical, functional, and psychosocial. The purpose of measurement in the clinical domain is to determine if the patient's physical health status has improved, stayed the same, or deteriorated. Symptom management, occurrence and severity of disease complications, degree of energy or fatigue, and intensity of experienced pain are common clinical measures.

The functional domain includes measures that evaluate mobility, self-care, household management, resumption of usual activities of daily living, return to work/school, limitations resulting from pain or other disabling symptoms, and patterns of sleep and rest.

Psychosocial indicators assess psychiatric or psychological symptoms; emotional states; cognitive and emotional responses to the symptoms, diagnosis, treatments, and prognosis of the presenting illness; feelings of self-esteem and self-efficacy; social functioning (for example, nature and quality of interpersonal relationships, appropriateness of interactional behaviors and patterns, and so forth), and recreation/pastimes.

Using this framework of three key outcomes measurement domains, a group of health services researchers in England developed measures to evaluate the outcomes of ambulatory health care services provided to patients with asthma and diabetes. They identified the following nine stages in their design of outcomes measures:

1. Specification of the relevant dimensions of health;

2. Review and selection of available health status and outcomes measures that address the specified dimensions of health;

3. Assessment of the sensitivity and discriminatory power, reliability, and validity of the selected measures;

4. Rejection of those measures that do not meet the requirements for acceptable performance;

5. Identification of the general health perception items from the retained measures;

6. Identification of items in the retained measures that examine specific health dimensions (for example, physical function, mental health, social function, and so forth);

7. Examination of the relationship(s) between general health perceptions and specific dimensions of health;

8. Statistical analysis of the correlation between general health perceptions and self-ratings on specific dimensions of health; and

9. Creation of the outcomes measures for management of asthma and diabetes in ambulatory care settings.[4]

In discussing contemporary outcomes research, Wilkins, Lowery, and Smith emphasize the expansion of outcomes measures beyond the traditionally evaluated mortality rates and morbidity classification and occurrences. A shift toward understanding the consumer's viewpoint has resulted in measures that focus on health status, quality of life, functional capacity, and overall quality of the episode of care.

The combination of health status and quality of life measures assess the overall impact of health care interventions on the patient's daily life. Many generic and disease-specific instruments can be used to evaluate health status and quality of life. The Functional Assessment of Cancer

Therapy, FACT, (representing breast, prostate, lung, and other malignancy versions) and the sickness impact profile for low back pain are examples of disease-specific instruments. The Short Form (SF) 36 and the Nottingham health profile are common generic questionnaires. The MOS-36 simultaneously assesses health status and well-being by using 36 questions in seven subscales: physical functioning, bodily pain, role limitations as a result of health problems, emotional well-being, social functioning, energy/fatigue, and general health perceptions.

Measures of functional capacity may evaluate impairment and/or disability. Impairment is commonly defined as demonstrable anatomical or physiological damage. Disability refers to the limitations that result from impairment. Standardized instruments that evaluate functional capacity typically focus on disability. An example is the RAND Corporation's physical capabilities index (PCI), which examines the effects of the illness and treatments on the patient's ability to perform common daily tasks.

Because pain and somatic symptoms so pervasively influence quality of life, functionality, and perceived health status, numerous instruments have been created to evaluate experienced pain and bodily symptoms. The pain drawing instrument and linear analog scale both evaluate chronic pain. The modified somatic perception questionnaire (MSPQ), which includes 22 self-report items, assesses a broader range of physical complaints.[5]

Generic health outcomes measures can be differentiated from disease-specific outcomes measures. General health outcomes measures are applicable to different diagnostic categories and treatment approaches. Many generic outcomes instruments are available. The Medical Outcomes Study 36-Item Short Form (SF-36), the Dartmouth COOP Charts, the Quality of Well-Being Scale (QWB), and the Sickness Impact Profile (SIP) are the generic health measures most frequently used in ambulatory care research. Collectively these measures, which assess a broad range of health concepts that are applicable across patient groups, are known as "measures of health-related quality of life" (HRQOL). The HRQOL includes measures of biopsychosocial well-being and impairment and disability. The advantage of using this group of instruments is that they include, but are not limited to, assessments of physical health and disease.

Disease-specific outcomes measures are useful for defined groups of patients with common diagnoses and similar symptoms. Because these tools detect clinically important changes, both patients and clinicians are keenly interested in the information they generate. Most of the measures available for ambulatory care research are disease-specific. Examples of useful instruments include the New York Heart Association (NYHA) Functional Classification, the Rose Questionnaire for angina, and the Oswestry Disability Questionnaire and the Roland Low Back Pain Disability Questionnaire, which both assess dysfunction related to low back pain.[6]

Staff from the Carle Clinic in Illinois conceptualized outcomes measures in a slightly different way. They summarized three types of outcomes measures: biological, general health, and disease-specific. Biological measures are focused on the physiologic functioning of organs and organ systems. Typically associated with a specific disease, such measures apply to the diagnostic and treatment monitoring components of the health care process. General health measures examine the health-related aspects of life that are relevant to all recipients of care regardless of particular traits or diagnoses. These measures typically evaluate physical capacity and functioning, mental health, social and role function and adaptations, and the patient's perception of his/her overall health. Disease-specific measures focus on the patient's symptoms and experiences in conjunction with a specific disease or diagnosis. Common areas for assessment include condition-specific symptoms, impairment, and disability and/or treatment-focused side effects and complications.

Outcomes studies often employ different types of measures to examine outcomes in different health domains. The five domains of health outcomes enumerated by these researchers and clinicians are clinical end points, functional status, general well-being, patient satisfaction, and service utilization and costs of care.

Measurements in the clinical end points domain yield subjective and objective data. Both the patient and the health care provider perspectives are reflected. Specific symptoms and complications of discrete disease states are elicited.

The functional status domain assesses the patient's ability to respond to the demands of daily living. Of particular interest to health care consumers, measures of functional status demonstrate the impact of disease and treatment on everyday life. Because functional status data are not always consistent with clinical data, measures that uncover both types of information should be used.

General well-being, as a domain of health outcomes, is also of great importance to patients. Well-being is a self-perceived state, therefore measurement of well-being produces highly subjective data. Self-perception of well-being is often examined in relation to service and resource consumption as health care seeking behaviors frequently result from feelings of discomfort and disease. A sense of well-being is also linked to successful adaptation to chronic illness. As such, correlating the degree of the patient's functionality with self-determined level of well-being is beneficial.

The satisfaction domain continues to gain greater importance in the current health care environment. Satisfaction measures examine the health care consumer's perceptions, thoughts, attitudes, and feelings about the health care system. Satisfaction measures also reveal patient expectations and requirements for a particular episode of care.

The service utilization and cost of care domain is the most challenging to measure. Current accounting systems are often structured in ways that make it difficult to capture true costs of care and accurately track resource consumption. The wide-ranging variation in the costs associated with managing seemingly similar health care conditions may represent actual differences in the cost of care. This variation may also be a reflection of inconsistencies and errors in measurement activities. In any case, the lack of definitive knowledge about the cause(s) of variability of health care costs confounds the ability to make meaningful decisions about the resources necessary to provide sufficient health care services.[7]

In the economic, clinical, and humanistic outcomes (ECHO) model of outcomes measurement, economic outcomes are the direct, indirect, and intangible costs of alternative treatments. Such medical, nonmedical, and indirect costs must be examined in relation to clinical and humanistic outcomes. Medical results of disease(s) and treatment(s) reflect clinical outcomes. Clinical measures indicate physical and/or psychological status, which is then used to determine the degree or severity of pathology and disease. Humanistic outcomes describe the effect of disease or treatment on the patient's functional status and quality of life.

When applying the ECHO model, the specific data that are collected are determined by different needs of data users. Utilization data collected for use by a managed health plan would typically include relative effectiveness of treatment, patient office and emergency department visits, use of laboratory tests, medical monitoring activities, personnel use and time, and direct costs associated with medication and supply usage. An employer making health plan purchasing decisions is commonly interested in the cost-effectiveness ratio of a health plan—how long it will take and how much it will cost to return an employee to the pre-illness level of work. Lost work time, return-to-work time, return to prior work activities, and quality of work are of critical interest when purchasing health benefits programs. Outcomes data of interest to physicians and other primary care providers include efficacy and advantages of different treatments, patient compliance, time spent with patients, and numbers of patients seen. The patient, as the consumer of health care services and user of health outcomes data, is most often interested in achieved health status, functionality, and quality of life following treatment. Also of interest are out-of-pocket expenses, availability and accessibility of practitioners and treatments, and the quality of the patient-provider relationship.

Considering the ECHO model and the variety of outcomes data that can be collected, the following 12 steps are essential in the development of an effective outcomes measurement and improvement program:

1. Identify high volume and costly diseases that are subject to significant treatment variation.

2. Determine the demographics and comorbidities of patients with the identified disease states.

3. Specify the current treatment and intervention options based on a review of pertinent literature and practice standards or guidelines.

4. Conduct a review of resource utilization for these different treatment options.

5. Assign organization-specific costs for the identified resources.

6. Specify the desired outcomes. These may include reduction of disease severity, reduction or amelioration of symptoms, minimization of complications, increased quality of life, and improved functionality and productivity.

7. Identify and describe interventions that lead to the achievement of the desired outcomes. This may result in the generation of protocols, procedures, guidelines, and other tools to aid decision making.

8. Determine current (baseline) resource utilization.

9. Implement the chosen interventions according to any defined practice models.

10. Identify and analyze the outcomes achieved by implementing the selected interventions and treatments.

11. Review and evaluate this new outcomes program for effectiveness and feasibility.

12. Modify the program based on the review and evaluation.[8]

THOUGHT BREAK

■ *Consider the clinically focused measurement initiatives in place in your organization.*

■ *Are you conducting general health or disease-specific outcomes measurement initiatives? Why or why not?*

■ *Review the kinds of data that are being collected.*

■ *Do you routinely collect health status data? If so, how? If not, why not?*

■ *Does your organization assess patient functionality following treatment? If so, what have those data revealed about the clinical interventions delivered by your practitioners?*

■ *Think about the kinds of nonclinical data that are collected in your organization.*

■ *What do the nonclinical measures assess?*

■ *Is the assessment of financial performance a high priority?*

■ *How is financial success defined in your organization?*

Using a Balanced Performance Measurement Model to Evaluate Organization Performance

An ambulatory care organization is a complex system composed of interdependent clinical, support, administrative, and financial functions. These functions, either directly or indirectly, enable the achievement of the organization's mission through the accomplishment of key strategic and operational goals. Any effort to study and understand performance at the organization level must also examine the performance of these various critical functions. For this reason, an ambulatory care organization should strive to develop and use a balanced performance measurement model.

A balanced performance measurement model typically employs measures of clinical and nonclinical outcomes, processes, and structures. It also includes satisfaction measures that assess the perceptions and experiences of different vested parties. The objective of a balanced measurement model is to evaluate organization performance by examining key functions from multiple critical perspectives. The organization should seek input from patients, their significant others, staff, the surrounding community, purchasers, payers, and other interested parties. A balanced measurement model should elicit data and feedback about clinical performance, the performance of key administrative

Table 3-1. Characteristics of a Balanced Measurement Model[9]

A balanced measurement model

■ is linked to the ambulatory organization's mission, vision, values, and strategic plan;

■ is well communicated and understood by all staff;

■ contains a focused, manageable number of measures that target key (strategic) performance areas;

■ is technically sound, reliable, valid, and state-of-the-art;

■ is systematically reviewed and periodically revised;

■ provides information on performance levels and trends;

■ is aligned with and reflective of the organization's reward and recognition systems;

■ is developed with input from various stakeholders; and

■ is pilot tested within the organization and revised based on the pilot experience before ongoing implementation.

and business processes, the performance of employed staff and involved physicians, financial performance, and satisfaction levels. Table 3-1, above, lists the characteristics of an effective balanced measurement model. Table 3-2, page 34, offers a series of focused questions that a comprehensive, balanced measurement model for an ambulatory care organization should address.

Three types of outcomes data are central to a balanced measurement model: patient outcomes, provider economic outcomes, and outcomes of interest to different, specific payers. Patient outcomes data are essential for identifying excellent practices and effective interventions, as well as patient care problems. Provider economic outcomes data provide cost analysis and resource utilization information. Cost analyses identify the actual expense for providing services to specific types or groups of patients. Resource utilization specifies the organization resources that are consumed when providing care and services. The goal of monitoring economic outcomes is to be able to

predict the cost of care for a particular patient population. The model may also present specific outcomes data that are of interest to particular payers. Such information typically reflects the outcomes of care for a payer's population of patients. These data are often clinical and reflect both positive and negative changes in the patients' condition.[10] Table 3-3, pages 35–38, provides an example of different measures that might be included in a balanced measurement model for an ambulatory care organization.

THOUGHT BREAK

■ *Do you believe your organization has effectively implemented a balanced measurement model?*

■ *If so, how was this accomplished?*

■ *If not, what have been the roadblocks?*

■ *How can those obstacles be surmounted?*

Table 3-2. Components of a Comprehensive Balanced Measurement Model

1. *Health outcomes and functional status.* To what degree do the patients served
   - achieve clinical improvement, including symptom amelioration?
   - increase functional ability to maximal levels, return to usual routines of daily life, and self-report improvement?

2. *Patient perception of care and services (satisfaction).* How satisfied are patients and their significant others with the
   - overall care experience?
   - competence and compassion of staff?
   - availability of needed care?
   - accessibility to essential services?
      How satisfied are payers and purchasers that
   - the most appropriate care is provided at the lowest cost?
   - service recipients return to a maximal level of functioning?
      How satisfied are staff with the overall working environment?

3. *Clinical care processes.* Is the care that is provided
   - based on state-of-the-art practices?
   - reliably consistent?
   - appropriate and efficacious?
   - effective and efficient?
   - delivered competently?

4. *The operation of critical nonclinical processes.* Have the nonclinical processes that directly or indirectly support the delivery of care to patients been identified and examined for
   - effectiveness?
   - consistency?
   - efficiency?
   - comprehensiveness?
   - currency?

5. *Resource management.* Is
   - staffing adequate?
   - necessary on-the-job-training provided?
   - the availability of supplies and equipment predictably adequate?

6. *Financial performance.* Are
   - service utilization and resource consumption acceptable?
   - operating costs at acceptable levels?
   - variances between projected and actual expenses acceptable?
   - revenues-to-expense ratios acceptable?
   - investments performing adequately?

Table 3-3. Example of Balanced Measurement Model for an Ambulatory Care Organization

I. Patient Demographics
   1. % male/female
   2. Age range; average age
   3. Top five medical diagnoses
   4. % patients with: 1–2 diagnoses
                          3–5 diagnoses
                          more than 5 diagnoses
   5. Average number of visits
   6. % first time visits/return visits

II. Clinical Services Provided
   1. % acute problems
   2. % disease management for chronic conditions
   3. % health maintenance/disease prevention
   4. % patient/caregiver health education

III. Health Outcomes
   Generic
   1. % patients that report: complete recovery
                                 partial recovery
                                 no recovery
   2. % patients reporting an improved sense of well-being
   3. % patients demonstrating a positive response to treatment/improved health status (for example, improved lab results, decrease in pain/discomfort, vital signs within normal limits, positive changes on physical assessment, and so on)
   4. % patients experiencing treatment side effects
   5. % patients experiencing treatment-related complications

   Disease-Specific (Calculated for the top five medical diagnoses)
   1. % patients that report: complete recovery
                                 partial recovery
                                 no recovery
   2. % patients that report improvement of specific/primary symptoms:
       complete improvement
       partial improvement
       no improvement
   3. % patients reporting an improved sense of well-being
   4. % patients demonstrating a positive response to treatment/improved health status (for example, improved lab results, decrease in pain/discomfort, vital signs within normal limits, positive changes on physical assessment, and so forth)
   5. % patients that comply with prescribed self-management regimen
   6. % patients experiencing treatment side effects
   7. % patients experiencing treatment-related complications

IV. Functional Status Outcomes
   Generic
   1. % patients resuming usual activities of daily living:
       completely

continued on next page

Table 3-3. Example of Balanced Measurement Model for an Ambulatory Care Organization (continued)

       partially
       not at all

2. % patients experiencing long term limitations/disability
3. % patients experiencing undesirable changes in social and role functioning
4. Range and average "return-to-work/school-time"

Disease-Specific (Calculated for the top five medical diagnoses)

1. % patients resuming usual activities of daily living:
       completely
       partially
       not at all
2. % patients experiencing long term limitations/disability
3. % patients experiencing undesirable changes in social and role functioning
4. Range and average "return-to-work/school-time"

V. Patient Perception of Care and Services (Satisfaction)

Perceptions of Care and Services

1. % patients that rate the care they received as:
       outstanding
       very good
       good
       poor
       unacceptable
2. % patients that rate the competence of care providers as:
       outstanding
       very good
       good
       poor
       unacceptable
3. % patients that rate their relationship with the primary care provider as:
       very positive
       neither positive nor negative
       very negative
4. % patients that report their expectations were:
       met
       not met
5. Total number of patient complaints; number/% of patient complaints in the following categories:
       practitioner-related
       reception staff-related
       accessibility of needed services
       timeliness of care/service
       responsiveness
       billing, reimbursement, and payment issues
       physical environment

continued on next page

Table 3-3. Example of Balanced Measurement Model for an Ambulatory Care Organization (continued)

Patient Knowledge
1. % patients reporting understanding of their health condition
2. % patients reporting understanding of the medical management of their health condition
3. % patients reporting understanding of their self-care responsibilities

Patient Loyalty
1. % patients that would return for future health care needs
2. % patients that would recommend the organization/practitioners to family and friends

VI. Other Outcomes

Operational/Administrative
1. Average wait time from first call to first visit
2. Range and average of time interval between scheduled appointment time and actual contact with practitioner
3. Number of missed appointments
4. Number of/% patient-canceled appointments
5. Number of/% practitioner-canceled appointments
6. Number of/% patient-rescheduled appointments
7. Number of/% practitioner-rescheduled appointments
8. % inaccurate bills

Utilization Management
1. Total number of patients seen
2. Number of/% patients seen by practitioner
3. Average time spent with patient
4. Average time spent with patient by practitioner
5. Total number of diagnostic studies
6. % diagnostic studies by type:
   lab
   imaging
   invasive diagnostic procedures (subcategorized into % for specific procedures)
   other
7. % diagnostic studies by practitioner
8. % diagnostic studies by practitioner and type
9. % lab studies for ongoing monitoring of chronic conditions

Human Resource Management
1. Total number of staff
2. Number of/% staff by role and discipline
3. Number of/% staff in each category of the performance appraisal rating system
4. Average sick time usage
5. Staff attrition
6. Average tenure
7. Total number of staff vacancies
8. % staff vacancies by position

continued on next page

Table 3-3. Example of Balanced Measurement Model for an Ambulatory Care Organization (continued)

Financial Outcomes
1. Expense/revenue ratio
2. Budget variances
3. Staff salaries as a % of total operating budget
4. % reimbursement denials
5. Cost for supplies
6. Cost for pharmaceuticals and medications

VII. Key Process Measures
1. Comprehensiveness of documentation of identified patient problems and treatment plan
2. Timeliness of documentation of identified patient problems and treatment plan
3. Consistency of follow-up on abnormal lab tests
4. Timeliness of follow-up on abnormal lab tests
5. Accessibility of patient records
6. Adherence to infection control processes
7. After-hours availability of health services
8. After-hours accessibility of health services
9. Effectiveness of communications with patients regarding any pre-visit requirements (for example, dietary limitations, special preparations, and so forth)
10. Efficient protocol for investigating sentinel events
11. Effective protocol for investigating sentinel events
12. Appropriate procedures for managing medical emergencies

Measuring Satisfaction with Ambulatory Care Services

Multiple stakeholders are keenly interested in satisfaction with ambulatory care services. Numerous definitions of satisfaction, as it relates to quality of care, exist. Of particular interest is the categorization of patient satisfaction articulated by Zastowny, et al. They divide satisfaction into four dimensions:

1. Satisfaction with the processes of providing care;

2. Satisfaction with the health benefits resulting from an episode of care;

3. Overall satisfaction with the global health care experience; and

4. Personal cost-benefit, or the value of the specifically provided care processes and consequent outcomes.[11]

When satisfaction is conceptualized in this way, developing meaningful measures of patient perception of care and services (satisfaction) becomes possible. Routine, ongoing measurement of patient satisfaction provides the ambulatory care organization with a steady stream of information that is potentially useful for the continual redesign and improvement of critical patient-focused health services processes.

Provider organizations often develop patient satisfaction tools. Such an organization-specific instrument allows ambulatory care providers to focus survey questions around the unique aspects of their services or special interest areas. Although not yet as plentiful as other types of outcomes assessment tools, standardized satisfaction instruments are being developed. Examples of patient satisfaction tools relevant to ambulatory care are the Annual Member Healthcare Survey developed by the Group Health Association of America (GHAA) and the American Medical Group Association (AMGA) Patient Satisfaction Survey, which is completed by the patient during a medical encounter.

The Agency for Health Care Policy and Research (AHCPR) is developing a satisfaction survey for the Health Care Financing Administration (HCFA). HCFA will use this survey known as the Consumer Assessment of Health Plans Study (CAHPS), for all health maintenance organizations that have Medicare risk contracts.[7]

THOUGHT BREAK

■ *What are the major recommendations you would make to strengthen performance measurement in your organization?*

EXERCISE BREAK

Take a few moments to complete Worksheet #6: Examples of Performance Measures, which is on pages 147–150 in the Appendix. Part I will help you draft clinical measures that will be meaningful for your own ambulatory care organization. Part II will assist you to develop nonclinical outcomes measures pertinent to your organization. Part III will facilitate the creation of satisfaction measures for use in your organization. Part IV will help you identify financial measures relevant for your ambulatory care organization. You may also find the completion of this worksheet to be a useful component of a performance measurement effort.

Key Points

1. Sources for ambulatory care performance measures include professional literature, NLHI, ambulatory care delivery organizations, and professional associations.

2. Performance measures useful in ambulatory care evaluate patient outcomes related to health status, functionality and well-being, clinical and nonclinical organization functions, financial performance, and patient satisfaction.

3. The use of a balanced model of performance measurement helps to foster an integrated, wholistic evaluation of organization performance.

4. Assessment of satisfaction is an integral component of a balanced performance measurement model. When measuring satisfaction, the organization should solicit feedback about the treatment outcome, care processes, overall treatment experience, and value of the service.

References

1. O'Leary MR: *Clinical Performance Data: A Guide to Interpretation.* Oakbrook Terrace, IL, 1996.

2. Palmer RH, Hargraves JL: The ambulatory care medical audit demonstration project. *Medical Care* 34(9):SS12–SS28, 1996.

3. Cole L, Houston S: Integrating information technology with an outcomes management program. *Critical Care Nursing Quarterly* 19(4):71–179, 1997.

4. McColl E, et al: Developing outcome measures for ambulatory care—an application to asthma and diabetes. *Social Science Medicine* 41(10):1339–1348, 1995.

5. Wilkins E, Lowery J, Smith D: Outcomes research: A primer for plastic surgeons. *Annals of Plastic Surgery* 37(1):1–11, 1996.

6. Radosevich D: A framework for selecting outcome measures for ambulatory care research. *Journal of Ambulatory Care Management* 20(4):1–9, 1997.

7. Schraeder C, et al: Population-based research data as a means to address health outcomes. *Journal of Ambulatory Care Management* 20(4):39–46, 1997.

8. Ortmeier B: Conducting clinical and health economic outcome studies in an ambulatory setting. *Journal of Ambulatory Care Management* 20(4):10–16, 1997.

9. Sluyter GV, Martin MA: Measuring the performance of behavioral healthcare organizations: A proposed model. *Best Practices and Benchmarking in Healthcare* 1(6):283–289, Nov–Dec, 1996.

10. Andrusko-Furphy K, Warren M: Data re-use: An effective solution for outcomes data collection. *Infusion* pp 22–26, May 1997.

11. Zastowny T, et al: Patient satisfaction and experience with health services and quality of care. *Quality Management in Health Care* 3(3):50–61, 1995.

Chapter 4:

Selecting Performance Measurement Systems for Use in Ambulatory Care

---

This chapter does the following:

1. Defines a performance measurement system;

2. Summarizes performance measurement requirements (the ORYX initiative) for ambulatory care organizations;

3. Describes the Joint Commission's list of performance measurement systems;

4. Presents the Joint Commission's Framework for the Selection of Performance Measurement Systems; and

5. Delineates the Joint Commission's guidelines, developed in conjunction with the ORYX initiative, for selecting a performance measurement system.

What is a Performance Measurement System?

The need for organizations to demonstrate good outcomes has led to the development of performance measurement systems. Clinical outcomes reflect the patient's health status and functionality. Nonclinical outcomes refer to administrative or business results. Clinical

---

THOUGHT BREAK

■ *Think about your understanding of performance measurement systems.*

■ *How would you define such a measurement system?*

■ *What is it composed of?*

■ *Why would your organization want to use a performance measurement system?*

---

changes may be examined at the level of the individual patient or aggregated to the level of a group of patients. Nonclinical outcomes are typically reviewed at multiple levels within an organization. Critical to this understanding of outcomes is the recognition that the measurement of results leads to the evaluation of process effectiveness.[1]

The Joint Commission defines a performance measurement system as an interrelated set of process measures, outcomes measures, or both, that facilitate internal measurement data on performance over time and external comparisons of an organization's performance. In short, a performance measurement system is a vehicle for understanding processes and their corresponding results. Essentially, a performance measurement system compiles data that, when analyzed, yields specific, actionable information that can be used to alter the key care and operational processes that lead to patient and organization outcomes.

THOUGHT BREAK

■ *Think about the measurement initiatives in place in your organization.*

■ *Is most of your measurement based on the use of unique internal measures that have not been selected from a performance measurement system?*

■ *Have you selectively chosen some measure(s) from a performance measurement system without using the entire system?*

■ *Or are you using an organized performance measurement system for the collection of clinical outcomes data?*

■ *If you are using a performance measurement system, review how the selection and implementation of the system occurred.*

Moving from Thought to Action: Selecting a Performance Measurement System

The selection and use of a performance measurement system should be understood within the context of the Joint Commission's requirements for improving organization performance. Standards in the "Improving Organization Performance" (PI) chapter of the *Comprehensive Accreditation Manual for Ambulatory Care* (*CAMAC*) require

■ a planned, systematic, and organized approach to performance measurement;

■ collection of performance data that addresses process and outcomes related to patient care and organization functions;

■ systematic assessment of performance data using appropriate data analysis techniques, including statistical quality control (SQC) when pertinent;

■ internal and external comparative analyses of performance;

■ systematic performance improvement based on performance levels and the organization's strategic goals and priorities; and

■ measurement and assessment of the effect of improvement actions.

The selection and use of a performance measurement system will help to achieve compliance with all PI standards. The use of a performance measurement system is especially helpful in meeting the data analysis requirements specified in standard PI.4.1 and the comparative analysis intent of standard PI.4.2.

Conducting meaningful performance measurement, assessment, and improvement occurs through the implementation of a performance measurement and improvement plan. It is within this context that the commitment to outcomes measurement occurs. Once that commitment is made, a number of critical questions emerge. How do you determine precisely what your organization needs from a performance measurement system? How do you find pertinent performance measurement systems? How do you review and evaluate the different systems? How do you discover how well a particular system will meet your organization's priority needs? And ultimately, how do you select the performance measurement system or systems your organization will use?

Performance Measurement Requirements (the ORYX Initiative) for Ambulatory Care Organizations

The implementation of the revised accreditation process, including the collection and use of outcomes data, will be incremental. As of the printing of this book, the specific performance measurement requirements for accreditation (the ORYX initiative) for ambulatory care organizations have not yet been determined. It is anticipated that, once defined, these requirements will include

1. selection of one or more performance measurement systems and a required number of measures that address a specified focus area within the ambulatory care organization; and

2. submission of performance data.

Upon determining these new accreditation requirements, the Joint Commission will define an implementation timetable. Ambulatory care organizations will then be expected to comply with the new requirements, regardless of when each organization is due for its next triennial survey. Failure to meet these requirements could jeopardize accreditation status.

It is anticipated that the scope of measurement expected in each ambulatory care organization will be expanded in future years. Over time, organizations will likely be required to select additional measures.

Once the ambulatory care organization submits performance data, Joint Commission staff will use defined criteria to determine the need for any follow up actions. When the new accreditation requirements related to the ORYX initiative have been determined, the Joint Commission will provide ample notice to allow ambulatory care organizations sufficient time for compliance.

THOUGHT BREAK

■ *Review your organization's performance/outcomes measurement initiatives.*

■ *Determine what percentage of your patient population is reflected in these measurement activities.*

■ *Think about what you would need to do to expand your performance measurement so that it would increasingly evaluate outcomes for a larger percentage of your patient population.*

The Joint Commission's List of Performance Measurement Systems

The Joint Commission has already initiated performance measurement requirements in several accreditation programs. A review and analysis of those requirements will help to define compliance requirements for ambulatory care organizations. The following discussion presents issues that are currently *under consideration.* NOTE THAT THE SPECIFIC PERFORMANCE MEASUREMENT REQUIREMENTS FOR THE ORYX INITIATIVE FOR AMBULATORY CARE ORGANIZATIONS HAVE NOT YET BEEN DETERMINED.

Ambulatory care organizations may be required to select a performance measurement system from the Joint Commission's list of acceptable performance measurement systems. This list presents performance measurement systems that have signed a contract with the Joint Commission. The Advisory Council on Performance Measurement, a panel of national experts in performance measurement that was convened by the Joint Commission in 1995, defined the evaluation criteria. (See Table 4-1 on pages 44–45 for a list of Council members.) The determination of whether a specific performance measurement system meets the screening criteria is based on a self-report by the performance measurement system. Over time, criteria will become increasingly more stringent. Each performance measurement system will need to be re-evaluated against all new criteria which it may or may not meet.[2]

When selecting a performance measurement system, careful consideration should be given to whether it meets current criteria and will be able to meet future criteria.[2] Table 4-2, pages 46–50, presents these screening criteria as the Joint Commission's Framework for the Selection of Performance Measurement Systems.

In exploring this model of ongoing criteria-based evaluation of performance measurement systems, the Joint Commission has explained:

> Successful incorporation of various measurement systems into the accreditation process depends in large part on a strategy of progressive or staged implementation requirements. Having each system meet stringent participation criteria from the outset would effectively curtail participation by some systems already in use by health care organizations. On the other hand, rapid incorporation of measurement systems into the accreditation process without ensuring that they can provide useful and relevant data would not enhance the value of accreditation.[3]

With the increased demand to conduct comprehensive outcomes measurement, numerous vendors are developing measurement systems that have applications for ambulatory care organizations. While a number of these are already available, it is likely that more systems will be developed as the demand for performance measurement continues to escalate.

Table 4-1. Members of the Joint Commission's Advisory Council on Performance Measurement

Walter McNerney, MHA (Chair Emeritus)
Health Services Management Program
JL Kellogg Graduate School of Management
Northwestern University
Evanston, IL

Ivo Abraham, PhD, RN, FAAN
Principal
The Epsilon Group
Charlottesville, VA

Mary L. Barker (ex officio; representing Joint Commission Business Advisory Group)
Vice President-Employee Benefits Management
Baxter Healthcare Corporation
Deerfield, IL

Dennis Brimhall, MM
President
University Hospital, University of Colorado
Denver, CO

Gary Carter, FACHE (ex officio; representing state hospital associations)
President
New Jersey Hospital Association
Princeton, NJ

Arnold M. Epstein, MD (Chair, System Evaluation Subcommittee)
Professor and Chairman, Department of Health Policy and Management
Harvard School of Public Health
Boston, MA

Kathleen Goonan, MD
Senior Vice President of Health Affairs
Blue Cross & Blue Shield of Massachusetts
Boston, MA

Stephen Jencks, MD, MPH
Clinical Advisor
Health Care Financing Administration
Baltimore, MD

Kathleen Lohr, PhD (Co-chair, Measure Evaluation Subcommittee)
Program Director
Research Triangle Institute
Research Triangle Park, NC

George Lundberg, MD
Editor-in-Chief, Journal of the American Medical Association
American Medical Association
Chicago, IL

Clement McDonald, MD
Regenstrief Institute of Health Care
Indiana University Medical Center
Indianapolis, IN

Barbara J. McNeil, MD, PhD
Department of Health Care Policy
Harvard University Medical School
Boston, MA

David Nash, MD
Director, Office of Health Policy & Clinical Outcomes
Thomas Jefferson University Hospital
Philadelphia, PA

R. Heather Palmer, MB, BCh, SM (Co-chair, Measure Evaluation Subcommittee)
Director, Center for Quality of Care Research and Education
Harvard School of Public Health
Boston, MA

David B. Pryor, MD (Chair)
System VP for Information Services
Allina Health System
Minnetonka, MN

Elizabeth Saviola (ex officio; representing Joint Commission Business Advisory Group)
Division Manager of Health, Welfare, & Disability Plans Administration
AT&T
Morristown, NJ

Lisa Simpson, MB, BCh
Deputy Administrator, Office of the Administrator
Agency for Health Care Policy and Research
Rockville, MD

John Ware, Jr, PhD
Senior Scientist, New England Medical Center
The Health Institute
Boston, MA

continued on next page

Table 4-1. Members of the Joint Commission's Advisory Council on Performance Measurement (continued)

John W. Williamson, MD
Director, Salt Lake RMEC (11R)
VA Medical Center
Salt Lake City, UT

Douglas Wood, MD
Vice Chairman, Department of Medicine
Mayo Clinic and Foundation
Rochester, MN

David R. Zimmerman, PhD
Director, Center for Health Systems Research and Analysis
University of Wisconsin-Madison
Madison, WI

THOUGHT BREAK

■ *Consider how familiar you are with formal performance measurement systems.*

■ *Are you aware of systems that focus on ambulatory care practices?*

■ *Do you know of systems that have measures geared toward ambulatory services?*

■ *Can you identify systems that assess outcomes for the primary patient populations your organization serves?*

■ *What can you do to expand your knowledge of performance measurement systems with applications for ambulatory care organizations?*

Selecting a Performance Measurement System

Reviewing a large list of potential performance measurement systems can be a daunting task. How is it possible to decide which of the many performance measurement systems listed is the most appropriate and cost-effective for your specific organization? How can you make a wise selection? Begin by identifying the listed performance measurement systems that are applicable to ambulatory care. Then, using a planned and organized decision-making process, you can evaluate listed performance measurement systems applicable to ambulatory care. This evaluation

■ is objective;

■ is reliable and replicable;

■ is sensitive;

■ differentiates performance measurement systems from one another; and

■ is thorough and consistent.

Figure 4-1, page 51, presents a specific process, a sequence of activities, for choosing a performance measurement system(s).

Identify your Organization's Measurement Goals

The selection of a useful, applicable performance measurement system must be predicated on a clear and present knowledge of your organization's goals for performance measurement. Use the following steps as you strive to define these measurement goals:

1. **Consider your organization's mission.** Why does your organization exist? How does it contribute to the community? How is your organization different from other ambulatory care organizations in the area?

2. **Review your organization's strategic plan.** What areas has your organization targeted for growth? To what areas are resources allocated? What high priority/high impact areas do your strategic and operational plans emphasize?

3. **Describe the patient population your organization serves.** What demographics characterize your patients? What specific services do you provide? Which services, treatments, and clients are high risk, high cost, high volume, problematic, or of some particular interest to your organization or the surrounding community?

Table 4-2. The Joint Commission's Framework for Selection of Measurement Systems

Note: *Although performance measurement requirements for accreditation for ambulatory care have* **not** *yet been determined, these criteria can be helpful in evaluating and selecting a performance measurement system that an ambulatory care organization may wish to use to enhance its measurement and improvement efforts.*

The Advisory Council on Performance Measurement agreed that, to be useful within the Joint Commission's accreditation process, all qualifying performance measurement systems must include seven elements called *Attributes of Conformance.*

The Framework identifies the title of each attribute. Each of the seven attributes is supported by two to eight criteria, for a total of 33 criteria. Each criterion specifies how and when the systems must satisfy the requirement.

The Joint Commission does not expect all performance measurement systems to immediately and fully meet all 33 evaluation criteria before being approved for inclusion in the accreditation process. Therefore, 19 criteria have been designated as requiring current compliance. These criteria are followed by the phrase "initial screening requirement" in parentheses. Fourteen criteria have been slated for future application. These criteria are followed by the phrase "required by (month/year)" in parentheses. A specific month and year are designated for each of these criteria.

ATTRIBUTE 1

Performance Measure Characteristics: Refers to characteristics of the performance measures submitted by measurement systems for use in the ORYX initiative.

Criterion 1A - Each performance measure submitted by the measurement system for the ORYX initiative is a *defined process or outcome measure.* (**Initial screening requirement**)

Criterion 1B - Each performance measure submitted by the measurement system for the ORYX initiative addresses at least one of the following performance categories: clinical, health status, patient perception of care, administrative/financial. (**Initial screening requirement**)

Criterion 1C - Performance measures submitted by the measurement system for the ORYX initiative do not address *individual practitioner performance.* (**Initial screening requirement**)

Criterion 1D - Each performance measure submitted by the measurement system for the ORYX initiative is related to at least one of the following Joint Commission accreditation programs: Ambulatory Health Care, Behavioral Health Care, Home Care, Hospital, Long Term Care, Pathology and Clinical Laboratory Services. (**Initial screening requirement**)

Criterion 1E - Each performance measure submitted by the measurement system for the ORYX initiative is reported as a *single rate* (that is, not reported in multiple stratification categories). (**Initial screening requirement**)

Criterion 1F - For each measure submitted for the ORYX initiative, measurement systems provide participating health care organizations with *pre-defined specifications,* including data element definitions, recommended data sources, population identification rules, calculation algorithms and, if appropriate, sampling protocols. (**Required by 7/98**)

continued on next page

Table 4-2. The Joint Commission's Framework for Selection of Measurement Systems (continued)

Criterion 1G - The measurement system has documented procedures for adding, modifying, maintaining and deleting performance measures. **(Required by 1/2000)**

ATTRIBUTE 2

Database (Measurement System Technical Capabilities): The operational characteristics of measurement systems.

Criterion 2A - The measurement system has at least one *automated database.* **(Initial screening requirement)**

Criterion 2B - The measurement system is *currently operational.* That is, the system (product) being submitted for the ORYX initiative
- is not currently in pilot testing;
- currently has at least two actively participating clients (or one client if an external database is used to construct a performance measure feedback comparison group); and
- has provided actively participating health care organizations with feedback, based on at least three months (one quarter) of post pilot test data, comparing performance across health care organizations [see Attribute 5]. **(Initial screening requirement)**

Criterion 2C - The measurement system is *ongoing.* That is, the system does not have a defined end date as in a demonstration project. **(Initial screening requirement)**

Criterion 2D - The measurement system currently *links* individual health care organizations or sites *with their own data* (that is, database contains health care organization identifiers). **(Initial screening requirement)**

Criterion 2E - The measurement system receives and stores, or can electronically access through participating health care organizations, *performance measure data at the level of individuals* (individual patient, enrollee, employee, and so on) for measures submitted for the ORYX initiative, in order to be able to transmit the required data elements to the Joint Commission (for example, measure standard deviation—see ORYX Technical Implementation Guide). [Measurement systems will not transmit data at the level of individuals to the Joint Commission. They will, however, be required to transmit data elements, such as standard deviations, calculated by the system from individual-level data.] **(Required by 7/98)**

Criterion 2F - The measurement system has plans in place to ensure that all databases and software supporting the product submitted for the ORYX initiative will be *"Year 2000" compliant.* **(Required by 1/99)**

ATTRIBUTE 3

Performance Measure Accuracy: The extent to which performance measures correctly identify the events they were designed to identify.

Criterion 3A - The measurement system monitors and is accountable for ensuring the *accuracy* and *completeness* of the performance measure data elements it receives from participating health care organizations and transmits to the Joint Commission. **(Initial screening requirement)**

Criterion 3B - The measurement system provides *ongoing support* to participating health care organizations to ensure that the accuracy of performance measure data elements is *monitored by the health care organizations.* **(Initial screening requirement)**

continued on next page

Table 4-2. The Joint Commission's Framework for Selection of Measurement Systems (continued)

Criterion 3C - The measurement system has established the *accuracy of the algorithms* used to calculate the performance measures submitted for the ORYX initiative. **(Required by 7/98)**

Criterion 3D - The measurement system has established that the performance measures submitted by measurement systems for the ORYX initiative are able to *consistently identify the events they were designed to identify* across multiple individual participating health care organizations. (For example, performance measure specifications are consistently applied across all participating health care organizations so that the same measures are collected in the same way.) **(Required by 7/98)**

Criterion 3E - The measurement system uses the results of performance measure accuracy monitoring to continuously improve the measures. **(Required by 1/2000)**

ATTRIBUTE 4

Risk Adjustment / Stratification: A process for reducing, removing, or clarifying the influences of confounding patient factors that differ among comparison groups.

Criterion 4A - The measurement system provides information on how it controls for the influences of confounding patient factors on performance measures submitted for the ORYX initiative. For performance measures that are currently risk adjusted, methodologies and techniques for reducing or removing the influences of confounding patient factors are described. For performance measures not currently risk adjusted, an explanation is provided for why the influences of confounding patient factors have not been addressed. **(Initial screening requirement)**

Examples of factors that patients might bring to an encounter and for which risk adjustment might be utilized include, but are not limited to,

- complications (conditions arising after the beginning of observation and treatment that modify the course of patient illness and the medical care required);
- co-morbidities (pre-existing diseases or conditions);
- severity of illness classification (for example, *AJCC staging* for oncology patients, *ASA-PS classification for* surgical patients);
- health status (for example, physical functioning, role disability due to physical-health problems, bodily pain, general health perceptions, vitality, social functioning, role disability due to emotional problems, and general mental health); and
- patient demographics (for example, age, ethnicity, and gender).

Criterion 4B - Performance measures submitted by the measurement system for the ORYX initiative are risk adjusted, if appropriate, to reduce or remove the influences of confounding patient factors so that valid and fair comparisons can be made across health care organizations. **(Required by 1/2000)**

Criterion 4C - Each performance measure to which risk adjustment applies has a unique risk adjustment approach tailored to it. **(Required by 1/2000)**

ATTRIBUTE 5

Performance Measure-Related Feedback: Performance measure-related information that is available, on a timely basis, to health care organizations participating in the measurement system, for use in the organization's ongoing internal efforts to improve patient care and organization performance.

continued on next page

Table 4-2. The Joint Commission's Framework for Selection of Measurement Systems (continued)

Criterion 5A - The measurement system (product) being submitted for the ORYX initiative routinely (minimum of once a year) provides, and actively participating health care organizations regularly receive, *performance measure-related feedback* (for example, paper reports, electronic database access) *comparing performance across health care organizations.* (**Initial screening requirement**)

Criterion 5B - The measurement system (product) being submitted for the ORYX initiative has provided actively participating health care organizations with feedback, based on at least *three months (one quarter) of post pilot test data,* comparing performance across health care organizations. (**Initial screening requirement**)

Criterion 5C - The measurement system makes *educational resources* available to help health care organizations understand and use performance measure data. (**Initial screening requirement**)

Criterion 5D - The measurement system is currently capable of providing individual health care organizations with comparative ORYX performance measure data on their organization no later than *the time those data are transmitted to the Joint Commission (that is, quarterly).* (**Required by 1/99**)

Criterion 5E - *External databases* used by the measurement system to calculate comparisons on performance measure data, or as a source of data transmitted to the Joint Commission for the purpose of making comparisons, include data that are less than two calendar years old (for example, during any part of 1998, data from any part of 1996 would meet the requirement.) (**Required by 1/2000**)

ATTRIBUTE 6

Relevance for Accreditation: The extent to which performance measurement systems are useful and relevant in the accreditation process.

Criterion 6A - The measurement system provides *statistically valid comparison groups* on each performance measure selected by accredited health care organizations to meet ORYX requirements. Each measure selected by health care organizations to meet ORYX requirements includes data representing a minimum of ten organizations in its comparison group. (**Required by 1/2000**)

Criterion 6B - The measurement system is prepared to assist the Joint Commission with the development and implementation of research-based methodologies for conducting evaluative studies. These studies assess the extent to which the performance measures selected by health care organizations to meet ORYX requirements are useful and relevant to the accreditation process (for example, degree to which performance measures are: discriminatory; useful for developing probes for use by surveyors; useful for reaching accreditation decisions). (**Required by 1/2000**)

ATTRIBUTE 7

Technical Reporting Requirements: Requirements related to the transmission of accredited health care organization data to the Joint Commission by performance measurement systems.

Criterion 7A - The measurement system is currently capable of electronically *transmitting* updated ORYX performance measure *data directly to the Joint Commission on a quarterly basis.* That is, quarterly data transmission to the Joint Commission originates from the measurement system, not individual health care organizations. (**Initial Screening Requirement**)

continued on next page

Table 4-2. The Joint Commission's Framework for Selection of Measurement Systems (continued)

Criterion 7B - The measurement system is currently capable of transmitting updated ORYX performance measure data to the Joint Commission in the form of *monthly data points*. **(Initial Screening Requirement)**

Criterion 7C - The measurement system is currently capable of transmitting *aggregated health care organization-level* data *and aggregated comparison group* (across health care organizations) data to the Joint Commission. **(Initial Screening Requirement)**

Criterion 7D - The measurement system is currently capable of transmitting performance measure data to the Joint Commission as a *single rate* (a proportion or ratio) or as a *continuous variable* (a measure of central tendency). **(Initial Screening Requirement)**

Criterion 7E - *Comparison group data* on individual performance measures transmitted by the measurement system to the Joint Commission, are consistently and continuously derived from the same pre-specified data source. (For example, a comparison group, such as a national, regional, state or local pool of health care organizations, is constructed and consistently used for reporting purposes.) **(Required by 7/98)**

---

4. **Identify your organization's specific performance improvement priorities.** What areas has your organization designated for improvement? What kinds of requests for performance information do you receive from patients, payers, purchasers, accreditors, regulators, competitors?

By focusing on these trigger questions, you will be able to identify where in your organization performance measurement is needed and will produce high-impact information. Failure to conduct such a deliberate assessment of measurement goals may result in the misallocation of measurement resources. Measuring too little or too much are both risks that can be tempered by gaining organization consensus on measurement goals. Only after measurement goals are defined is it possible to specify what and how to measure. Only then does the sound choice of a performance measurement system become possible.

Establish a Clear and Objective Evaluation Process

It is important to think, plan, and document how your organization will evaluate and select a performance measurement system(s). Follow these steps to develop your plan:

1. **Identify who in your organization should participate in the performance measurement system selection process.** Will you have an executive sponsor for this process? Who should make the performance measurement system selection recommendation(s)? Who will ultimately make the final selection decision? Have you involved the staff who will use the measurement system in the decision-making process? If your organization is a part of a larger health care system, explore what performance measurement systems other organizations in your system have selected or are considering.

2. **Identify the criteria that your organization will use to select a performance measurement system.** What measures must your performance measurement system include? What technical support does your organization need? What special and specific requirements does your organization have for a performance measurement system? Under what constraints is your organization laboring?

3. **Determine if all your selection criteria are equal in importance.** Are some evaluation criteria more important than others? Do some criteria identify "must haves" and

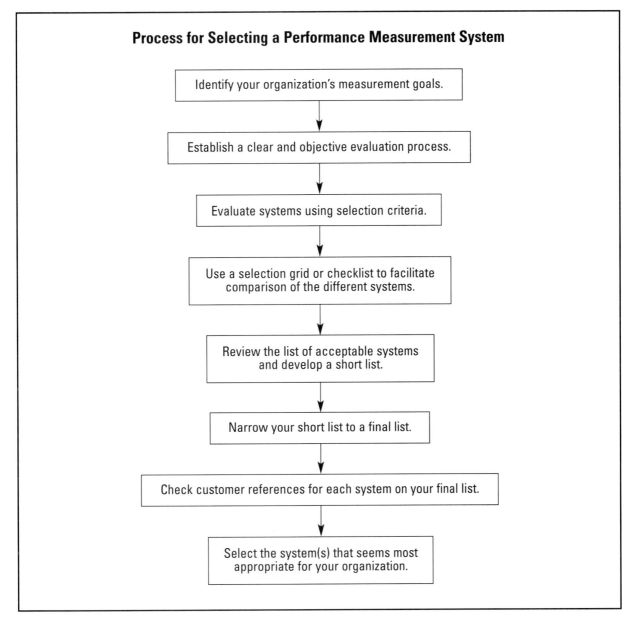

Figure 4-1. *This flowchart presents a specific process for choosing a performance measurement system.*

other criteria identify "nice to haves?" Should you weight the criteria, giving more decision-making importance to those crucial must have items?

4. **Create a performance measurement system selection plan that specifies time lines and milestones.** What critical path must you follow to select and begin using a performance measurement system? How do you need to schedule choosing a performance measurement system so that your organization can meet the Joint Commission's time requirements? What critical decision points must you address in a timely way? Do you need to build in any "slack" on the critical path of your project management plan?

Implementing your performance measurement system evaluation plan should result in a recommendation for use of one or more performance measurement systems. Some organizations may elect to use only one system, others may opt to use multiple performance measurement systems. By using a planned and systematic approach to evaluating the performance measurement systems, you can ensure that your recommendation is based on fact, rational examination, and critical analysis.

Evaluate Systems Using Selection Criteria

Identifying what your organization requires from a performance measurement system is crucial. Each ambulatory care organization may have unique needs and place emphasis on different areas. As you develop selection criteria, you should do the following:

1. **Distinguish between required and desired performance measurement system characteristics.** What criteria are essential to your organization meeting its critical performance measurement needs? What criteria are so crucial that the failure of a performance measurement system to meet those criteria results in an immediate decision to remove that system from further consideration? What nonessential characteristics would you hope your recommended performance measurement system has? Will you weight criteria to differentiate importance or necessity?

2. **Clearly define your organization's requirements for performance measurement system capabilities.** What technical capabilities does your organization need? Will you be mandated to upgrade your information system or hardware? What is the cost of ongoing service contracts? Are price increases expected? What are your organization's data management, data analysis, and data/information reporting needs? Will your data be sold to others? What human factors must the performance measurement system address? How much assistance will your organization want from the performance measurement system?

3. **Use the Joint Commission's Framework for the Selection of Performance Measurement Systems** (Table 4-2, pages 46–50) **to help you assess the various performance measurement systems.** How well do the performance measurement systems in which your organization is interested meet the Joint Commission's criteria? Does your organization want to include any Joint Commission criteria in your selection criteria? (All Joint Commission criteria, except those listed under Attribute 6, could be readily included in your list of required or desired criteria.)

Using the Joint Commission's framework criteria. It is reasonable to use all available resources to help your organization define its performance measurement system selection criteria. The Joint Commission's Framework for the Selection of Performance Measurement Systems (Table 4-2), developed by national experts, reflects some of the most contemporary advice on selecting performance measurement systems. By employing this framework as a part of your selection criteria, you will assess each performance measurement system's status against attributes defined by experts in outcomes measurement.

It is important to remember that the presence of a performance measurement system on the Joint Commission's list means it meets the criteria with current dates; it does not provide quantitative information on how well it meets the criteria, nor are the systems asked to indicate if they meet future criteria. It is, therefore, important to examine each performance measurement system's status on each criterion. The following information may help you successfully complete that task:

Attribute 1: Performance Measures. Criteria 1A through 1G focus on the types of measures included in the performance measurement system and their relevance to Joint Commission accreditation programs.

When selecting measures, consider asking the following criteria-based questions:

- Does the system include clinical, perception of care, and health status measures?
- Does the system identify the health care delivery setting to which each measure relates?

Knowing the applicability of the system's measures to Joint Commission accreditation programs will assist you with the Joint Commission's requirement to select measures relevant to your patient population.

Criteria 1F and 1G discuss the extent of documentation for and definition of each measure in the system and the relationship of measures to the Joint Commission's accreditation programs. The documentation of definitions increases the likelihood that participants are in fact measuring the same thing. Without that assurance, comparative information could be suspect. The information derived from your participation will be used by the Joint Commission to evaluate your performance, by your organization to identify improvement opportunities, and perhaps by others to purchase or select care. In other words, important decisions about your organization will be made based on the exact data you collect. This criterion also stipulates that the specific directions (algorithms) for determining the occurrence of the event described by the measure are documented.

Consider asking the following criteria-based questions:

- Does the system provide definitions of the measures, including the populations of interest (denominator) and the events being measured (numerator or measurement)? Ask to see examples.

- Is the intent or rationale for each measure described?

- Which measures has the system identified as available to meet Joint Commission requirements?

- Do you have the option to use only the measures of interest to your organization, or must you use the entire set provided by the system?

- Are the data elements that comprise the measures listed and defined, including allowable values for each?

- What are the sources of the required data? Systems that use only claims data often do not capture important clinical data for calculating or risk-adjusting measures of clinical care.

- Are directions for sampling provided when applicable?

You may also want to ask if the performance measures have been field tested to ensure that data can be captured completely, accurately, and consistently by provider organizations.

Criteria 1F and 1G increase the likelihood of providing valid, comparative information to participants because the system has better data-auditing and risk-adjustment capabilities (patient-level data), and the review of data for each patient record is accomplished through the use of a defined, standardized algorithm.

Attribute 2: Database (Measurement System Technical Capabilities). Criteria 2A through 2D are current requirements and list several points related to the database itself. Each listed system has indicated that it has an operational, automated, centralized database. Because there are different types of databases, you may still want to ask whether it is centralized, stores your data separately from those of other participants, and supports intraorganization and interorganization comparisons. In addition, ask the system whether it is capable and willing to send your data to the Joint Commission on your behalf. Other questions you may want to consider asking include the following:

- How is the integrity of the database maintained?

- How are the confidentiality of, and access to, the database protected?

- Can you have access to the database? If yes, how? If no, why not?

- How are data submitted and stored in the database (paper, diskette, modem)?

- If your organization must collect and submit data manually, will the system accommodate data submitted on paper?

- Are there certain time lines, restrictions, and rules associated with data submission?

- What is the technical structure and capacity of the database?

- What are the qualifications of the technical staff?

- Is there a support structure (for example, help desk) for your use?

These details can provide insight about the longevity of the database and flexibility to support your continued data submission and participation. The number of enrollees will also affect the database. Therefore, it is important to determine if the system has adequate volume to provide meaningful comparative data.

Additional questions you may want to consider asking include the following:

■ How many organizations currently participate in the system?

■ How large is the database now? How many patient cases are actually in the database?

■ What expectations does the system have for new enrollment? On what is this based?

■ What has been the growth pattern of the database?

■ How will the database continue to meet participants' needs if there is significant new enrollment?

Criterion 2E is a current requirement and addresses the need for systems to have access to performance measurement data at the level of individuals. Criterion 2F is a future requirement addressing system readiness for Year 2000 compliance.

Attribute 3: Performance Measure Accuracy. The five criteria under this attribute address the accuracy and completeness of performance measurement data. Criteria 3A through 3C and 3D address the system's auditing practices and support provided to participants to ensure data accuracy and the measures' validity. Currently, a system should have an audit process in place, the results of which are shared with users. In the future, the system will also need to demonstrate that

■ the results of data checks are used to improve the quality of the data;

■ calculations of measures are accurate; and

■ measures are identifying all events that should be captured by the measure.

The following questions might be asked of system representatives:

■ Does the system regularly check the quality of submitted data? Ask the system representative to describe the process to you.

■ Does the participating organization receive feedback about its own particular data quality problems?

■ Are general data quality problems shared with all participants?

■ Are the results of the data checks shared with participants?

■ Can you correct and resubmit your data?

■ Does the system use audit results to make changes to the measures and data elements?

■ Are there clear directions (algorithms) for calculating the measures?

■ Were the measures field tested for the above characteristics?

■ Does the system provide a mechanism for assuring that a sufficient number of participants have selected a measure to generate statistically meaningful reports?

■ Are current participants actually identifying improvement opportunities?

■ To what organization or clinical functions do the measures relate?

Criterion 3B focuses on the system's provision of education and ongoing support as related to data quality issues. Systems should be currently providing this type of education and support. In the future, systems will be expected to monitor the quality of data at the individual participant level. The following questions might be asked of system representatives:

■ Is education about data quality issues provided to participants? Ask for a description of this service.

■ Are participants expected to submit to the system the results of their own internal data audits? If not now, how will the system meet this future criterion?

■ Are users' groups held?

■ Is support documentation provided to users?

■ Can you get assistance from the system to improve the quality of your data?

Attribute 4: Risk Adjustment/Stratification. It cannot be stressed strongly enough that today's health care environment is characterized by the movement toward accountability and measurement. Your organization will likely be asked, if it has not been already, to provide data for use by various publics to make judgments and decisions about your organization. Even your own use of comparative data will drive resource investments into particular care processes of concern.

Therefore, it is important to know that your performance is compared fairly to other participants who are using the same measure from the same system. The comparisons must be fair, believable, and actionable when necessary. Fair comparisons are facilitated by risk adjusting the measure to consider the severity and complexity of the patient's condition, or, when appropriate, by stratifying the rates according to particular patient characteristics, such as age or gender, that are known to be related to the outcome being measured.

Criterion 4A, an initial screening criterion, expects systems to explain the process for risk adjusting or stratifying measures, as well as provide a rationale for those measures that are not risk adjusted or stratified.

To assess this criterion, consider asking these questions:

- Does the system include any measures describing events that may be confounded by patient factors, such as demographics, comorbidities, severity of illness, or functional status?

- If yes, ask how the patient factors are identified to adjust participants' rates.

- What statistical techniques are used to adjust data?

Criteria 4B and 4C expect that, in the future, particular types of measures will be risk adjusted or stratified uniquely.

- If the system does not risk adjust or stratify rates, ask for an explanation as to why it does not and what its plans are for future use of such techniques.

Attribute 5: Performance Measure-Related Feedback. Access to individualized, timely, comparative reports is the primary reason you are participating in a performance measurement system. You can collect meaningful data of high quality, but they must be turned into comparative information and provided to you in a timely manner to be useful. Use of this additional information will help you achieve the ultimate goal of performance measurement—performance improvement. This attribute describes expectations related to the feedback provided by the system to participants.

Criterion 5A, a current criterion, expects that participants who are actively submitting data receive comparative feedback. A system must be able to provide valid comparisons across its participants. Ask if the system can currently meet this criterion.

Criterion 5B, also current criteria, states that this feedback is based on data that are updated at least annually (current criterion) and, in the future, updated according to the Joint Commission's transmission schedule (quarterly). Frequent provision of reports will help you find connections between data and current care processes.

For example, we would all agree that a useful outcomes measure for oncology treatment is long term survival. Today's five-year survival rate, however, is in part the result of the processes of care provided five years ago—a situation you cannot change today unless the identical processes are still in place. Similarly, feedback provided to you today that is more than one year old may not be meaningful in identifying processes needing to be improved.

To further assess Criterion 5B, consider asking the following questions:

- How often are reports provided?

- How timely are they?

- How are risk-adjusted rates displayed?

- What is the report turnaround time from data submission to report receipt?

- How are reports provided to you—hard copy through the mail or electronically?

- What type of support does the system provide to help you interpret the reports?

- Does the system publicly disclose your data?

- Does the system allow you to share the data (reports) with other users if you so choose?

- Will the system assist you with disclosing data to others?

- Are ad hoc reports available? If so, at what cost?

- Does the system and database support benchmarking?

- Do high-level performers disclose their rates and participate in a true benchmarking experience with participants?

Criterion 5C, also a current expectation, addresses the system's capability to provide education and interpretation support to participants. Ask the system representative how this support is provided.

Criterion 5D, a future requirement, relates to whether the system is prepared to provide participating health care organizations with data in the same form as such data are transmitted to the Joint Commission at the same time.

Criterion 5E, also a future requirement, relates to the age of the data being used to generate comparative metrics.

Attribute 6: Relevance for Accreditation. For the system to be integrated into the Joint Commission's accreditation process, it must meet two specific criteria. Both are marked for future compliance.

Criterion 6A addresses the system's ability to send system-level data that allows the Joint Commission to view an individual health care organization's rates against other health care organizations using the same measure. In order for comparisons to be useful and meaningful, they must be statistically valid. The Joint Commission has provided measurement systems with specific information about required system-level data elements. This is a future criterion since data submission is not yet required. You want to select a system, however, that assures you it will be able to meet this expectation.

You might consider asking the following questions to evaluate a measurement system's ability to meet Criterion 6A:

■ Can the measurement system demonstrate the statistical validity of the comparisons generated for the measures your organization is interested in using?

■ Will the comparison group for each measure your organization is interested in using include data representing a minimum of ten organizations?

Criterion 6B stipulates that the system work with the Joint Commission to design and conduct evaluative studies. These studies will be an ongoing part of the evolution of the new

accreditation process. This is also a good place to ask about the system's current agreement with the Joint Commission.

Attribute 7: Technical Reporting Requirements. Comparisons of performance across health care organizations will be interpretable over time only if they are regularly generated from the same pre-specified comparison group. If an external or third-party comparative database is used, it is important that comparisons be generated on data from the same time period. At a minimum, the most current data in an external comparative database must not be more than two years old.

To evaluate whether a measurement system meets these criteria, you might consider asking the following questions:

■ What is the comparison group for each measure?

■ Will the comparison group remain constant for the period of time your organization expects to use the measure?

■ Will your organization's performance be compared to data from an external database (for example, state data tapes, census data, claims/insurance data)?

■ Will comparisons be made against data collected during the same period of time?

■ How old are the most recent data in the database for the measure(s) you are interested in using?

Each listed system has signed a contract with the Joint Commission indicating its commitment to remain in compliance with current criteria and its intent to meet future criteria. *You are strongly encouraged to discuss these issues with the system representative as well.*

Use a Selection Grid or Checklist to Facilitate Comparison of the Different Systems

Selection grids and checklists are tools to enhance decision making. A selection grid may help you to compare and contrast the attributes of multiple performance measurement systems. Such a selection grid would

■ list the performance measurement systems you wish to evaluate;

- enumerate your required and desired criteria;
- specify the weight of each criterion; and
- have empty cells in which you can document the
  - total number of points for a particular criterion, and
  - overall score for each assessed performance measurement system.

Figure 4-2, page 58, provides an example selection grid for reviewing and scoring performance measurement systems.

A checklist is a visual aid that can help you compare and contrast, at a glance, the attributes of different performance measurement systems. Such a checklist specifies

- the performance measurement systems you wish to evaluate, and
- your required and desired criteria.

Figure 4-3, page 59, provides an example checklist for reviewing performance measurement systems.

Review the List of Acceptable Systems and Develop a "Short List"

It would be virtually impossible, unrealistic, and even unnecessary for an ambulatory care organization to intensively evaluate every performance measurement system on the Joint Commission's list. Therefore, it is desirable to rapidly narrow the large list into a short list that will be subject to more intensive analysis. The first step in creating this short list is to compare each performance measurement system you are considering to your required criteria. Eliminate any systems that fail to meet these criteria.

Next, examine the total complement of measures for each performance measurement system that meets your required criteria. Although performance measurement requirements for accreditation do not yet apply to ambulatory care, you may wish to give special attention to those performance measurement systems listed as acceptable for meeting the performance measurement accreditation requirements. Look

for a written description of the purpose and intent for each measure in each system on your short list. If this is lacking, consider eliminating that system from your list of possibilities.

Review Table 4-3, pages 60–61, which describes characteristics of performance measures. Then ask the following questions about each performance measurement system that initially meets your required criteria:

1. Does it include measures that match our needs?
2. Does it include measures that are relevant to our measurement goals?
3. Does it include measures that will help to identify improvement opportunities in the services we provide and the health care outcomes we achieve?
4. Does it measure processes and outcomes that we can affect?
5. Will we be able to implement the measures?
6. Are the measures and their data elements defined precisely and specifically?
7. Can the measures accurately define the events they were designed to define?
8. Will the measures yield data that we can interpret and translate into meaningful and useful information?
9. Is the comparison group for each measure clearly defined and pertinent to our organization?
10. Will we be able to communicate the performance measure results to interested parties relatively easily?
11. Does or will this system likely meet our future performance measurement needs?
12. Does or will the system produce data that we can use to meet other requirements, such as benchmarking or public disclosure of performance?

If in reviewing a specific performance measurement system, you are unable to answer yes to most or all of the above questions, seriously consider eliminating that system from your roster of potential performance measurement systems.

If one or more of your key stakeholders has recommended performance measurement systems

Selection Grid for Reviewing and Scoring Performance Measurement Systems

Reviewed by: _____

Directions: Starting with the must-have criteria, check the criteria met by each system in the left-hand column. If a system meets all the must-have criteria, proceed to the next level of review against the desirable criteria. Each desirable criterion is followed by its weight in parenthesis. Then, score the degree to which a system meets each criterion. The criterion score should be placed in the lightly shaded box below the criterion. Multiply this score by the weight assigned to the criterion to arrive at the weighted score for the criterion. Place the weighted score in the box below the criterion score. Total the weighted scores for each system and put this number in the last column. Every system that meets the must-have criteria and has an acceptable total on the desirable criteria should be checked against the Joint Commission's Framework criteria.

System Name	Obstetrical indicator	Release of data to public allowed	Affordability	Measures addressing clinical, patient satisfaction, health status, and/or administrative financial aspects (Joint Commission current criteria)	Operational, ongoing database (Joint Commission current criteria)	Ability to submit data electronically directly to the Joint Commission (Joint Commission current criteria)	Installs on mainframe (3)	Provides regional analysis (2)	Has documented procedures for adding, modifying, maintaining, and deleting measures (3) (Joint Commission future criteria)	Total of Weighted Scores
System A	X	X	X	X	X	X	4 / 12	5 / 10	3 / 9	31
System B	X		X	X	X					
System C		X	X	X	X					
System D	X	X	X	X	X	X	5 / 15	4 / 8	3 / 9	32
System E	X	X	X	X	X	X	4 / 12	4 / 8	2 / 6	26
System F	X	X								

Must-Have Criteria		
	Desirable Criteria	

Key

Weight
1 = Somewhat Important
2 = Important
3 = Very Important

Score
0 = Does Not Meet
1 = Will Meet
2 = Minimally Meets
3 = Partially Meets
4 = Substantially Meets
5 = Fully Meets

Figure 4-2. *This sample selection grid for reviewing and scoring performance measurement systems illustrates how this tool can be used to help track and compare your evaluations of performance measurement systems. Your organization's selection grid would include all your established must-have and desirable criteria.*

Checklist for Reviewing Performance Measurement Systems

Reviewed by: _____

For each system, check criteria met by system.

Must-Have Criteria	System A	System B	System C	System D	System E	System F
Obstetrical indicator	X	X		X	X	X
Release of data to public allowed	X		X	X	X	X
Affordability	X	X	X	X	X	
Measures addressing clinical, patient satisfaction, health status, and/or administrative/financial aspects *(Joint Commission current criteria)*	X	X	X	X	X	
Operational, ongoing database *(Joint Commission current criteria)*	X	X	X	X	X	
Ability to electronically submit data directly to the Joint Commission *(Joint Commission current criteria)*	X			X	X	

IF A SYSTEM MEETS ALL MUST-HAVE CRITERIA, PROCEED WITH THE NEXT LEVEL OF REVIEW CRITERIA

Desirable Criteria	System A	System B	System C	System D	System E	System F
Installs on mainframe	X			X	X	
Provides regional analysis				X	X	
Has documented procedures for adding, modifying, maintaining, and deleting measures *(Joint Commission future criteria)*	X			X	X	

Figure 4-3. *This sample checklist for reviewing performance measurement systems illustrates how this tool can be used to help track and compare your evaluations of performance measurement systems. Your organization's checklist would include all your established must-have and desirable criteria.*

Table 4-3. Characteristics of Performance Measures

Because performance measures are the heart of a performance measurement system, consider evaluating potential systems against the following characteristics of measures as you develop your short list. These characteristics are offered as general, helpful guidelines, not as rigid rules to follow.

■ *The system includes performance measures that are relevant to your organization's measurement goals.*

■ *The system includes performance measures that can identify opportunities for improvement in the services you provide and the quality of the health care results you achieve.* Health care organizations use performance measurement data to improve care provided to patients, better understand the processes of care, identify problems with current processes, and manage risk. To achieve any of these objectives, your organization will want to select measures that can raise good questions about the processes you currently have in place and the outcomes from these processes. Good questions are those that identify opportunities for improvement in the quality of the health care services you provide. Measures should also assist you in prioritizing your organization's improvement activities by identifying areas that have the greatest need for positive change. Ultimately, the measures you select must tell you whether improvements have occurred in your organization's processes and patient outcomes.

In addition, the performance measures you choose should help identify and reward investments that produce results important to your organization and its stakeholders. For example, performance measures could monitor the effects of a postdischarge follow-up process initiated to track surgical site infections. Results indicating that hospital readmissions decrease and patient satisfaction increases if infections are prevented or identified and treated early would support continued resource investment for such a follow-up process for discharged patients.

■ *The system includes performance measures that monitor processes and outcomes your organization can affect.* There is little value in collecting data on processes or outcomes over which your organization and providers have little or no control. You must be able to influence the processes and outcomes tracked by any performance measure you use. However, in some cases, your organization's ability to influence specific health care-related processes and outcomes will not be known until changes are implemented and their effects measured.

■ *The system includes performance measures that your organization can reasonably implement.* The cost and ease of implementing performance measurement will vary by individual performance measure and by individual organization. For example, some measures might be more easily collected by a large organization with automated data collection capacities; other measures may be more easily collected by a small organization using manual data collection processes. You will want to adopt measures that are feasible to implement while still providing valuable information. The most feasible measures

— can be calculated with available data;

— can be calculated with data you already collect in electronic format;

— can be interpreted at the level of frequency that the measured event occurs in your organization (for example, the needed sample size to interpret some measures may not be readily achievable in a small organization);

— minimize the overall data collection burden;

— can be implemented and used for a reasonable cost; and

— can be collected while maintaining appropriate confidentiality of any patient information.

continued on next page

Table 4-3. Characteristics of Performance Measures (continued)

■ *The performance measures and their data elements are precisely defined and specified to ensure uniform application.* For performance measurement data to be useful, they must be comparable across health care organizations; and in order for data to be comparable, their data elements must be defined and collected and the measures calculated in the same way each time. Therefore, performance measures must have precisely defined populations, data elements, allowable values, calculation algorithms, and, where applicable, sampling procedures.

Activities directed at ensuring performance measure accuracy include the implementation of data quality processes for data collection, entry, retrieval/reporting, and verification of integrity. These activities help ensure the reliability of the data collected. You should be sure the measure produces the same results when repeated in the same populations and setting and can be applied consistently across multiple settings and organizations.

■ *The performance measures can accurately identify the events they were designed to identify.* Only performance measures that accurately identify the events they were designed to identify will be useful to your organization or its stakeholders. A performance measure must correctly identify the occurrences or cases meeting its defined conditions (true positive cases), as well as the individuals or cases not meeting its defined conditions (true negative cases).

■ *The performance measures produce data that can be interpreted and transformed into meaningful and useful information.* To provide useful information to your organization, performance measures must be able to identify changes in performance over time and variation across organizations or settings. For any measure, this requires that enough cases are included in the sample to statistically detect variation over time and across comparison groups. If your needs are complex, you may want to consult with a statistician on how best to ensure adequate sample sizes.

Also, for most outcome measures and many process measures, some type of risk adjustment may facilitate comparison and interpretation. That is, they may benefit from analytic processes for reducing or removing the influences of confounding patient factors that differ among comparison groups of participating health care organizations. Some examples of patient factors that might confound comparisons and on which measures could be risk adjusted are comorbidities, severity classifications, pre-existing health status, and patient demographics, such as age or ethnicity.

■ *Performance measure results can be communicated to interested parties.* Performance measure results must be reportable in a manner that is useful to your organization and other interested stakeholders. Examine the measurement system's feedback reports to see if they will meet, or usefully supplement, your organization's reporting needs.

to you, consider including those systems on your short list for more intensive scrutiny.

You must consider required resource allocations when narrowing down your large list of potential performance measurement systems. Try to determine what resources must be invested to purchase and maintain the performance measurement system. Consider the following:

1. Initial implementation expenses, including

   a. costs for purchasing the system;

   b. costs for new hardware;

   c. costs for new software;

   d. staff resources for installation, custom programming, and other miscellaneous activities; and

   e. training costs.

2. Annual operating expenses, including

   a. staff resources for collection, submission, and use of data;

   b. any ongoing user fees; and

   c. training costs.

Eliminate those performance measurement systems with costs that are prohibitive for your organization.

If you are currently participating in a performance measurement system that is on the Joint Commission's list, add it to your short list as well. You can then evaluate whether it will continue to meet your future measurement needs.

Finally, remember that some measurement systems are "niche" players. They are designed to measure processes or outcomes in specific areas, such as ambulatory surgery, obstetrics and gynecology, renal dialysis, or physical therapy. Consider including such systems on your short list if they apply to your organization.

It may take time and effort to develop your short list. It is time well spent, however, because it will limit the number of extensive, in-depth reviews you will have to do.

Narrow Your Short List

You now have a short list of performance measurement systems that appears to be

- able to meet your current and future measurement needs;
- usable with reasonable effort;
- within your budget parameters and resource limitations;
- of interest to a variety of stakeholders; and
- in alignment with your organization's required criteria.

The challenge now is to further narrow your short list and select one system. You can accomplish this task using a selection grid. By using a point-based approach you can evaluate each of the performance measurement systems on your short list against your final selection criteria. An explanation of how you might do so follows.

First, *weight each final selection criteria* according to its level of importance. A three-point weighting system might specify the following:

    1 = Somewhat Important;

    2 = Important; and

    3 = Very Important.

Second, *assign a scaled score* for each final selection criterion. A scaled score indicates the degree to which each performance measurement system on your short list meets each final selection criterion. A six-point scoring system might specify the following:

    0 = Does Not Meet;

    1 = Will Meet In The Future;

    2 = Minimally Meets;

    3 = Partially Meets;

    4 = Substantially Meets; and

    5 = Fully Meets.

Third, *calculate the total criterion score* for each final selection criterion. The formula for calculating the total criterion score is as follows:

Selection Criterion Weight	X	Selection Criterion-Scaled Score	=	Total Criterion Score

The following example illustrates the weighting and scoring of a *specific selection criterion* applied to three different performance measurement systems:

Your organization will select a performance measurement system that uses the same type of information technology you currently use. This is one of your final selection criteria. You weight this selection criterion 3 (Very Important). If Measurement System X successfully runs on a system identical to yours, you would assign a selection criterion scaled score of 5 (Fully Meets). If Measurement System Y can run on your system with some modifications, you would assign a selection criterion scaled score of 3 (Partially Meets). If Measurement System Z cannot run on your current system and will require a totally new system, you would assign a selection criterion scaled score of 0 (Does Not Meet).

The Total Criterion Score for System X is 15:

Selection Criterion Weight	X	Selection Criterion-Scaled Score	=	Total Criterion Score
(3)	X	(5)	=	(15)

The Total Criterion Score for System Y is 9:

Selection Criterion Weight	X	Selection Criterion-Scaled Score	=	Total Criterion Score
(3)	**X**	**(3)**	**=**	**(9)**

The Total Criterion Score for System Z is 0.

Selection Criterion Weight	X	Selection Criterion-Scaled Score	=	Total Criterion Score
(3)	**X**	**(0)**	**=**	**(0)**

Fourth, after calculating the total criterion score for every final criterion and each performance measurement system on your short list, *calculate the performance measurement system score.*

The Sum Of The Total Criterion Scores For A Performance Measurement System	=	The Performance Measurement System Score

Total Criterion A Score
+
Total Criterion B Score
+
Total Criterion *n* Score
=
The Performance Measurement System Score

Figure 4-4, page 64, provides an example of a point-based selection grid you might use to score each performance measurement system on your short list against your final selection criteria.

Fifth, *rank in order* from highest to lowest score.

Sixth, *shorten this rank-ordered short list to a final list.* (Where to draw the cut-off point is largely a judgment call. It is typical, however, for one or more natural breaks to occur among items on a rank-ordered list. You may use such natural break points to help you decide which perform-ance measurement systems you will include in and eliminate from your final list.)

Finally, *review your final list against the Joint Commission's Framework Criteria,* presented on pages 46–50. You may wish to design a selection grid (similar to the one in Figure 4-2) that will allow you to assess each of the performance measurement systems on your final list in relation to the Joint Commission's current and future criteria.

Check Customer References for Each System on Your Final List

Thoroughly investigate the performance meas-urement systems on your final list. Ask for an on-site demonstration at your own facility. Try to obtain a demonstration copy of the software and experiment with it for several weeks.

Visit or contact an ambulatory care organization that is already using the performance measure-ment system. Ask them the following questions about their experiences working with the system:

- How well does it work?
- What is the quality of customer support?
- What was their installation experience like?
- How valuable has the system actually been in meeting their performance measurement goals?
- After having used the system, would they purchase it again? Why or why not? Would they encourage other organizations to pur-chase the system? Why or why not?

Select the System or Systems that Seem Most Appropriate for Your Organization

You have learned a great deal about the final few performance measurement systems that are of interest to your organization. It is time to recommend and purchase the performance measurement system(s) that will be of greatest benefit to your organization.

The performance measurement system(s) you choose will likely meet all your required (must have) criteria. Conversely, all your desired (nice to have) criteria will likely *not* be met. The sys-tem you purchase today may or may not meet all the Joint Commission's future criteria.

As with any other decisions you make, you must weigh the strengths and weaknesses of each alter-native choice. You must examine the cost/benefit of each different selection. In the end, you must simply make the most objective, informed choice that you can. The comprehensive performance measurement system review process in which your organization engaged can help you do just that:

Point-Based Selection Grid for Evaluating Performance Measurement Systems on the Short List Against Final Selection Criteria

Performance Measurement System	Final Selection Criteria					Performance Measurement System Score
	1 (SCWT)	2 (SCWT)	3 (SCWT)	4 (SCWT)	5 (SCWT)	
	SSCS: TCS:	SSCS: TCS:	SSCS: TCS:	SSCS: TCS:	SSCS: TCS:	
	SSCS: TCS:	SSCS: TCS:	SSCS: TCS:	SSCS: TCS:	SSCS: TCS:	
	SSCS: TCS:	SSCS: TCS:	SSCS: TCS:	SSCS: TCS:	SSCS: TCS:	

KEY:

SCWT = Selection Criterion Weight
(1 = Somewhat Important, 2 = Important, 3 = Very Important)

SCSS = Selection Criterion Scaled Score
(0 = Does Not Meet, 1 = Will Meet In The Future, 2 = Minimally Meets, 3 = Partially Meets, 4 = Substantially Meets, 5 = Fully Meets)

TCS = Total Criterion Score (SCWT multiplied by SSCS)

Performance Measurement System Score = Sum of all Total Criterion Scores (TCSs) for each performance measurement system

Figure 4-4. *This selection grid provides a format that can be used to objectively evaluate performance measurement systems on your short list against final selection criteria. Completion of the grid will help to identify those systems that should receive in-depth analysis.*

choose a performance measurement system that best meets your current needs and has the promise of continuing to meet your future needs.

EXERCISE BREAK

Take some time now to complete Worksheet #7: Action Plan For Evaluating And Selecting A Performance Measurement System, which is on pages 151–152 in the Appendix. Creating this action plan will help you specify what steps need to be taken in what time frame for your organization to meet the Joint Commission's performance measurement requirements (the ORYX initiative). You may find it helpful to bring a draft of this document to a meeting of your top management or quality oversight body for discussion, reaction, and revision.

Key Points

1. A performance measurement system is a structured tool for collecting and analyzing data. It allows for internal and external comparisons. It may also be viewed as a warehouse of outcomes information.

2. Performance measurement requirements under the ORYX initiative have not yet been determined for ambulatory care organizations.

3. The Joint Commission will make available a list of performance measurement systems that, by self-report, meet the applicable criteria in the Joint Commission Framework for the Selection of Performance Systems.

4. The Joint Commission Framework for the Selection of Performance Systems delineates initial and future screening criteria that an ambulatory care organization can use to

facilitate an objective evaluation of prospective performance measurement systems.

5. A thorough and objective process for evaluating and selecting a performance measurement system involves several key steps:

   a. Identify measurement goals;

   b. Define an objective, criteria-based evaluation process;

   c. Develop and use organizing tools, such as checklists and selection grids, to aid decision making;

   d. Narrow a lengthy list of possible systems into a smaller list of options by systematically eliminating those systems that least comprehensively address your measurement needs;

   e. Check customer references; and

   f. Make a judgment-based decision in selecting the most appropriate performance measurement system for your organization.

References

1. Meffort J: Order in a new era: Outcome documentation. *CARING Magazine* pp 18–23, Jun 1996.

2. Joint Commission on Accreditation of Healthcare Organizations: *Using Outcomes To Improve Performance In Long Term Care and Subacute Care Settings.* Oakbrook Terrace, IL, 1997.

3. Loeb JM, Buck AS: From the Joint Commission on Accreditation of Healthcare Organizations. *Journal of the American Medical Association* 275(7):508, Feb 1996.

Chapter 5:

Designing and Implementing an Outcomes-Based Performance Improvement Project

This chapter does the following:

1. Explores how to design an outcomes-based performance improvement project;

2. Suggests ways to successfully manage the data generated by a performance improvement project;

3. Explains how to use an outcomes-based performance improvement project to improve organization performance; and

4. Emphasizes the need to communicate essential project-related information to various interested audiences.

Project Design

Successful performance improvement projects result in improvement—the achievement of better outcomes and more effective and efficient processes. Given a truly supportive organization environment, the planned and thoughtful design of each specific outcomes-based performance improvement project is the single greatest contributor to that project's success. An improvement project should not be launched until its goals have been defined, scope has been specified, resource needs have been determined, constraints have been identified, problems have been anticipated, and success measures have been established. An early investment in such project planning affords an organization the opportunity to proactively design the project for real strategic impact.

Describe the Specific Outcomes Measurement Project

Dedicate, at the outset of the outcomes measurement project, as much time as is necessary to create a comprehensive project plan. The plan should function as a "project road-map," outlining movement from the current situation to the desired future state.

Explore the origin of the project. Document how the project was identified. Explain why it is of concern at this particular time and how it relates to the organization's strategic goals.

Clearly articulate the purpose(s) of the project. Summarize what the organization hopes to accomplish through this initiative. State, as concretely as possible, the desired "end products" and results of this specific effort.

Think of this project's anticipated impact. Then define the project's scope by deciding what processes and outcomes are contained within the project boundaries and which exceed those boundaries.

Explain how it will be known if this effort is successful. How will a change be shown to be an improvement? Develop and agree upon a few high-level measures of project success.

Determine what resources will be needed to effectively conduct this improvement effort. Identify the number, type, and time of personnel and related costs. Identify anticipated technological and equipment needs. Explore potential costs for benchmarking and customer evaluation. Define any specialized team training needs.

Research and clearly state any project constraints. Determine if specific resource limitations exist, either for the project itself or for the improvement changes it will generate.

Try to anticipate problems. Common challenges include staff resistance, knowledge deficits, fear of change, and inadequate leadership. Uncover, if possible, any unexpressed requirements or expectations about the types of changes that can be tested, recommended, and implemented.

Determine key project milestones and deadlines. Estimate when the root cause analysis will be complete, when the improvement ideas will be generated, and when the final report and recommendations will be available. Discuss how and when to provide intermediate project reports to the executive management. Consider whether such reports should be oral or written, given by the team leader or the entire team, or presented to the executive sponsor of the team or the entire quality oversight body. Agree upon the reporting protocol and indicate when the project reports will be delivered.

THOUGHT BREAK

- *Review how improvement projects are initiated in your organization.*

- *Who can recommend a project?*

- *How is the project proposed?*

- *To whom is the project proposed?*

- *How is the project approved?*

- *Once approved, how does an improvement project begin?*

- *What planning steps are taken to prepare for conducting the project?*

Assemble the Interdisciplinary Project Team

The synergistic, dynamic characteristic of an effectively functioning work team makes teams particularly popular vehicles for performance improvement. Although naturally occurring work teams are sometimes employed, more often organization leaders assemble temporary, project-focused, interdisciplinary teams and charge them with the responsibility of understanding and improving the performance of one or more dimensions of an important function, process, or outcome.

Such performance improvement teams are generally composed of four to eight individuals who work within, are customers of, or suppliers to the function or process targeted for improvement. In order to achieve a balanced, complementary, and comprehensive perspective on the team, the assigned members typically represent different clinical and nonclinical disciplines, clinical and operational areas, and staff levels within the organization. Significant effort should be expended to ensure that all functional areas related to the purpose and scope of the improvement project are represented on the project team. Each individual's participation on the team must be required by top leadership, endorsed by managers, and supported by coworkers.

Several distinctly important roles exist in performance improvement teams. The *sponsor* or "champion," as the role is sometimes called, is a member of the executive leadership and usually has line management responsibility for the organization area in which the improvement will be made. The executive sponsor has several important responsibilities, including

- expressing the executive vision of the improvement;

- providing senior management input and decision making, as necessary;

- serving as an information conduit between the team and the executive leadership;

- ensuring that needed resources are available;

- offering ongoing support and encouragement; and

- assisting with problem resolution as needed.

Sometimes the organization's quality oversight committee, which is usually composed of the executive leadership and the performance improvement director, serves as a guide for the project team. This committee's responsibilities are much like those of the executive sponsor and include

- expressing the executive perspective about performance assessment, the interdependence of key work processes, and the feasibility of proposed improvements, as they relate to the organization's strategic vision;

- overseeing the allocation of improvement resources;

- redirecting the team, if necessary;

- serving as an information conduit between the performance improvement team and line management; and

- providing approval for continued project efforts and proposed solutions.

Although not required, the *team leader* is often the mid-level manager with operational responsibilities for the work area in which the improvement will be made. The team leader must be knowledgeable about operations and outcomes in the area targeted for improvement. The team leader's responsibilities include

- gaining approval for and monitoring the improvement project budget;

- coordinating team meetings, including scheduling, preparing agendas, assigning project work to be completed between meetings, documenting team activities, and so forth;

- creating and monitoring the implementation of the improvement project work plan and time line;

- using and distributing the resources necessary to accomplish the team's charge;

- serving as an intermediary between the team and executive leadership;

- communicating regularly about the team's work with the team sponsor; and

- briefing and debriefing with the team facilitator before and after team meetings and at other times, as needed.

The team *facilitator* is usually a veteran staff person with excellent interpersonal skills and no line management accountabilities in the operational area targeted for improvement. Effective facilitators are experienced and educated in work team dynamics and operations; performance improvement principles, practices, and tools; the organization's defined improvement process and chosen improvement methodology; performance measurement and assessment, including process and outcomes measurement and statistical process control techniques; and adult education. The facilitator's responsibilities include

- educating team members about the organization's selected performance improvement method, improvement tools and techniques, and performance measurement and assessment;

- helping the team create and sustain an effective working dynamic;

- coaching the entire team and individual members in the use of performance improvement tools, the collection and analysis of performance data, the generation and testing of improvement ideas, and the development of improvement recommendations;

- helping the team to prepare for formal presentations to the executive leadership;

- meeting with the team leader before and after team meetings to analyze the effectiveness of the team process and plan process interventions, if necessary; and,

- providing support and encouragement.

A *data consultant* may be part of the performance improvement team. This individual is often a member of the performance improvement resource staff, has extensive knowledge about data collection and analysis, may be a statistician, and may serve as the team facilitator or an ad hoc consultant to the team. In small organizations or those with minimal resources, consultation about data management can be sought from local university/college faculty, graduate students, and/or through related professional associations such as the American Society for Quality (ASQ) and the American Statistical Association (ASA). The responsibilities of the data consultant include

- providing guidance on determining data needs;

- assisting with the design or selection of data collection instruments;
- specifying statistical and nonstatistical data analysis techniques;
- assisting in data analysis/interpretation;
- guiding the pilot test of data collection and analysis; and
- providing education about data management, as needed.

Team *members* are the backbone of the team, completing the majority of the team's work. They are the staff whose daily work is affected by the area and issues targeted for improvement. Because of their empirical knowledge of the work being studied, they are often referred to as "subject matter experts." The critical responsibilities of the team members include

- attending team meetings regularly;
- participating actively in all team meetings;
- completing all between-meeting assignments;
- learning and using performance improvement tools and techniques, including performance measurement and assessment strategies;
- bringing issues, concerns, and problems to the attention of the team and team leader; and
- supporting and promoting the improvement project to peers and co-workers.

To optimize the team process, team membership should remain stable throughout the course of the improvement project. However, an outcomes-based performance improvement team sometimes needs input from staff not formally assigned to work on the specific improvement project. Such individuals may be thought of as "ad hoc" or "ex-officio" members of the team.

Summarizing the project in writing is helpful when designing an outcomes-based performance improvement project. Joint review of such a document by the executive leadership and the project team fosters a shared, common vision for the project, highlights any areas of confusion or misunderstanding, and defines the expected results of the project.

THOUGHT BREAK

- *Think about teaming for improvement at your organization.*
- *Review how teams are formed.*
- *How are individuals chosen to participate on improvement teams?*
- *Identify the typical team roles at your facility.*
- *How are team roles assigned?*
- *How are staff prepared for their team roles and responsibilities?*
- *How do you handle the need to engage other personnel not formally assigned to the improvement team?*
- *How are team responsibilities integrated with daily work activities and responsibilities?*

Outcomes-Based Performance Improvement: Considerations for Ambulatory Care Organizations With Limited Resources

Many health care professionals and ambulatory care organizations are committed to providing excellent patient care despite a paucity of resources. The clinicians, administrators, and other individuals who work in ambulatory care settings

- serve an increasing number of uninsured and underinsured patients;
- manage the health and health care of patient populations suffering from complex, chronic, multisystem medical problems and simultaneous environmental disadvantages;
- are dedicated to caring for socioeconomically deprived individuals and families;
- have few or no affiliations with larger health systems or networks;
- provide highly subspecialized care; and
- are staffed with a small number of personnel.

These individuals are no less interested in providing excellent patient care and service, nor less invested in the continuous improvement of their organization's performance than colleagues working in more resource-stable environments. Despite many limitations in these challenged settings, organization performance improvement is typically *not* stalled by lack of staff interest, commitment, or ability. But how can outcomes-based performance improvement be initiated and sustained in these ambulatory care organizations? Some strategic considerations follow. (See Chapter 2, pages 22–25 for additional suggestions.)

Be sure that 100% of your staff understands your organization's mission. Organization constancy of purpose and survivability are anchored in an enduring mission—the reason for the organization's existence, the definition of what the organization does. Staff must understand and be able to describe your ambulatory care organization's mission from both the patient and organization perspectives. Because **what** an organization does changes only infrequently, once a mission is understood it may need occasional clarification but will generally not need to be relearned. **How** an organization performs what it does frequently changes, usually in response to compelling internal and external forces. This stability of organization purpose and flexibility in the ways it is achieved are generally easy to understand but often difficult to accept. This is especially true when the change and flexibility affect the daily work activities of one or more staff. For this reason, organization leaders must offer frequent reminders that the ambulatory care organization can only maintain its ability to fulfill its mission by dynamically recreating itself in response to changing needs.

Work diligently to ensure that all staff understand that your ambulatory care organization is a purposeful system. An authentic and pervasive appreciation for your ambulatory care organization as an interdependent, integrated, goal-directed system is critical if staff are to understand why and how decisions are made. Once the purpose-driven, systemic nature of organizations is widely understood, decisions about priorities, goals, and activities at the organization and individual levels can be made more objectively and expediently; interpreted more universally; recognized

more accurately as attempts to optimize organization viability; and supported more consistently.

Focus on the true goal of performance improvement: the achievement of better outcomes. Performance improvement has become a powerful force in healthcare. However, the real reason for organization commitment to performance improvement and its techniques and processes is and should be to achieve improved outcomes: better health status, increased functionality, greater feelings of well-being, deeper levels of patient and stakeholder satisfaction, better patient and significant other perceptions of care and service, enhanced community standing and reputation, efficiencies in process operations, reduced resource consumption, fewer expenses, increased revenue, and improved profitability of the organization.

Be ruthless and rigorous in selecting performance improvement projects. Every possible improvement project cannot be initiated, and every worthwhile improvement project cannot be conducted. Only those improvement projects with the greatest potential for generating high impact results can be considered seriously. Any proposed performance improvement project that will not improve the organization's ability to achieve its mission, maximize its operation as a system, and increase the effectiveness and efficiency of its core work, should be rejected. Nonendorsement of a suggested improvement effort does not mean it lacks value or merit, nor does it imply that the recommendation was ill-conceived or inadequately developed. Elimination of potential projects is a business decision; a choice about resource allocation that is driven by the need to optimize overall system performance.

Commit only to strategic improvement projects. Making real organization improvements is often invigorating. Assuming responsibility for process change can be empowering. Not uncommonly, improvement projects are more interesting than the routine of daily work. Many compelling improvement opportunities exist. Those improvements that will have a direct effect on patients and families are especially enticing to practitioners. Improvements with immediate financial impact are particularly inviting to administrators.

Tremendous temptation to conduct multiple improvement initiatives exists. To successfully achieve meaningful improvements through a systematic, objective, and data-based process, however, you must limit the number and scope of improvement projects your organization conducts at any one time. Committing to more than can be realistically accomplished will result in an inability to complete many or all of the improvement efforts that are underway. This can lead to staff fatigue, frustration, anger, resentment, and devaluation of performance improvement in general, as well as disbelief in the value, benefits, and real commitment to performance improvement in your own organization.

Many organizations will conduct no more than four or five major, organizationwide, and strategic improvement projects in one year. Such broad scale improvement initiatives might include the development of clinical pathways or guidelines, redesign of the patient record, development of a new clinical service, design of a new employee compensation and benefits package, installation of a computerized information management system, evaluation and selection of a performance measurement system, and so on.

Determining the number and mix of improvement projects that an organization can effectively manage is more art than science. There are no hard rules. Perhaps the most sound advice is to start conservatively. You can always add additional initiatives. But calling a moratorium on a project already underway is very difficult. Remember, performing three important projects very well and achieving significantly improved results is better than performing six important projects incompletely and achieving sporadic and less than desirable levels of improvement.

Use staff prudently. It is tempting to engage each staff member in multiple high impact improvement projects. In so doing, more improvements can be made in less time with more employee involvement. Although this may be true in theory, it is not true in practice. Assigning too many projects to individual staff members depletes inner human resources such as energy, creativity, mental clarity, problem-solving skills,

and so forth. Furthermore, it can create an unmanageable workload which may produce an inevitable decline in performance of both regular work and special project work.

Encourage staff to participate in no more than two major improvement projects at a time. Urge them to dedicate no more than three to four hours each week to high impact performance improvement activities. Ensure that participation in improvement activities never interferes with the quality of patient care. For instance, avoid scheduling clinicians to see patients when they are planning to engage in specific improvement tasks that do not require patient involvement (such as collection of data from sources other than the patient, data management, data analysis, root cause analysis, generation of improvement ideas, and the like). Ensure that the reception desk and telephones are always attended. When staff with primary customer service functions leave their assigned areas to participate in performance improvement activities, institute a "coverage schedule" that requires other administrative and clinical staff to respond to the immediate nonclinical needs of patients.

Involve the appropriate individuals in improvement initiatives without convening large groups of staff in formal improvement team meetings. Although the facilitated, multidisciplinary, cross-organizational, and officially led improvement team is the most common (and perhaps most desirable) structure for conducting and completing improvement projects, it is not the only way to accomplish improvements. In ambulatory care organizations with severe constraints, assembling such teams is not always feasible. However, this should not prohibit or inhibit performance improvement. One or two staff may effectively bear responsibility for conducting a defined performance improvement initiative. They can be accountable for

- objectively determining and understanding the causes for current performance;
- communicating current performance levels and the reasons for these performance levels to colleagues;
- facilitating others' involvement in generating a list of focused actions that are expected to lead to better outcomes;

- planning for and conducting a test of the chosen, finite number of improvement actions under serious consideration;

- reporting the results of the pilot test(s) to colleagues;

- fostering consensus-driven decisions about what specific improvement actions to institute and how to implement them;

- creating final products and structures (such as new protocols, practice standards, policies, procedures, guidelines, and so on); and

- designing and implementing an ongoing performance monitoring process.

The success of this approach to performance improvement is contingent upon several key tactics:

1. Staff should only be assigned primary responsibility for improvement projects that are aligned with their expertise and that affect their area's functional responsibility and involvement.

2. The staff primarily responsible for each improvement project must also be accountable for its success. But because the organization's staff, as a whole or individually, can exert a powerful enabling or disabling force, every staff member is also responsible and accountable for the success of every improvement effort. These responsibilities and accountabilities must be explicitly and publicly stated.

3. The "unvarnished truth" must be valued. Staff must be empowered to examine their own work processes and performance as well as those of colleagues. All staff must believe in and support an open, nonjudgmental, and fearless discovery and analysis of performance.

4. Staff investment in specific performance improvement initiatives must be nurtured. Unguarded staff sharing and dialogue related to each improvement project must be solicited, understood, and considered. Conducting improvement projects in "isolation" and announcing changes to uninvolved co-workers must be avoided.

5. Each improvement project must be transparent. Expectations must be clearly defined and expressed. All staff must understand,

agree upon, and support the achievement of project goals and delivery of desired end products. Concerns, issues, and problems must be addressed openly, without criticism, and in a timely fashion. Hidden agendas must be recognized, acknowledged, revealed, discussed, and then eliminated.

Demand the consistent use of your chosen improvement method as the only way to systematically achieve performance improvements. Use of a single-disciplined and structured improvement method is central to the planned and systematic achievement of high impact, organizationwide improvements. It provides a common and familiar organization language for improvements while supporting an approach that is understood by all staff. It funnels staff time, attention, knowledge, and creativity toward deeply and accurately discovering and implementing changes that lead to improved outcomes and away from determining how to structure improvement initiatives and tasks.

You do not need to choose and use a complicated or lengthy improvement method. You are not required to adopt or adapt an existing improvement method. (Many organizations, especially those trying to stretch already stretched resources, find it practical to do so.) You are not obligated to use a method that is reliant upon computer applications or any other performance improvement tools or technologies.

However, your ambulatory care organization must use an improvement method that

- requires a factual understanding of performance;

- bases itself on the objective measurement and assessment of performance;

- demands a priority-based review and selection of potential improvement actions; and

- tests the effects of improvement actions before integrating them into normal process operations.

Educate all organization staff in your chosen improvement method and its use. Demand and hold one another accountable to the use of your chosen improvement method for all improvement projects. Do not expect or require sophisticated documentation and reporting of improvement activities. Instead, use simple forms and formats for documentation and reporting. Present information in bulleted points. Use graphics with short narrative explanations as much as possible. Distribute summary reports and make detailed reports available to those who are interested in reviewing them. Use existing communication structures, such as meetings, bulletin boards, e-mail announcements, and so on, to provide reports on improvement activities.

Conduct meaningful outcomes-based performance measurement and improvement despite resource limitations. The most sophisticated ambulatory care organizations often lack internally all the knowledge and skills to support comprehensive organization performance improvement. Even the most well-endowed organizations experience real resource limitations.

If you work in an ambulatory care organization operating "on a shoestring budget" with a small, tired staff of individuals "wearing four or five hats at one time," take pride in the significant contributions you and your colleagues make **despite serious constraints**. Your ability to focus on the most important work will serve you well in your performance improvement efforts.

Admit that finances and time limit your ability to make the types and numbers of improvements you would hope to achieve. Publicly acknowledge that you do not have all the desired performance improvement technical knowledge and skills within your organization. Commit to finding creative and innovative ways to infuse your organization with a new capability for performance improvement. The following are only a few of the many possibilities for doing so:

1. Many professional associations, health care specialty societies, health institutes, businesses with significant health care interests (such as pharmaceutical companies and manufacturers of medical supplies and equipment), private philanthropic organizations, and public entities have funds available to support quality of care research, efforts to evaluate and improve clinical/patient outcomes, and a variety of quality-related demonstration projects.

Search for these dollars. Review announcements in journals and newsletters. Contact your professional membership associations and ask if they have "seed" money or funds to support small quality of care studies. Talk with colleagues within and outside of the health care industry, asking if they are aware of available support money.

2. Faculty and researchers from academic health centers are frequently interested in forming partnerships with provider organizations. Academics typically have extensive knowledge about measurement and may have successful track records in securing grants. Often, they are aware of common and obscure funding sources. Many times, however, they do not have strong links to individual practitioners or provider organizations. This challenges their ability to conduct practice-based research.

Professionals working in health care delivery organizations are knowledgeable about how to provide the most contemporary care and treatment. They have awareness and experience of the real issues that affect and interfere with the ability to achieve optimal patient and organization outcomes. Typically, they have an intuitive sense of how to alter clinical and nonclinical processes in order to achieve more desirable results. Generally, their knowledge of research methods, measurement tactics, and statistical analysis is limited. Partnerships between academics and providers are win/win relationships because they exploit the unique strengths and compensate for the limitations of each partner.

Work actively to develop such relationships. Re-establish communication with mentors and favorite professors from your alma mater. Contact faculty from local universities and colleges. Facilitate discussions that help to clarify respective goals and identify shared objectives, exploring then the variety of ways in which you can work together productively.

3. Many retired or retiring professionals have led active and meaningful professional lives and remain interested in offering their leadership and contributing their experience and

knowledge. Often these individuals are enthusiastic about volunteering their services. They are typically mission-driven and committed to helping younger professionals learn from the accumulated experiences of their long and successful careers; they are truly an untapped "font of knowledge."

Seek out these individuals. Contact the speaker's bureau, public relations, or human resources departments of respected local health care organizations, businesses, universities, and professional schools. Explain your search for expert volunteer help. Ask them to direct you to possible sources of assistance. Use every professional and social engagement as an opportunity to educate others about your organization, its mission and priorities, and its needs for assistance.

Improving organization performance can be a struggle. Some ambulatory care organizations have very few resources to dedicate to any activities other than direct patient care. Staff in these settings often find creative, nontraditional ways to meet or exceed many important demands. Undoubtedly, the similar resource challenge to performance improvement can be addressed effectively with this same ingenuity and risk-taking spirit.

EXERCISE BREAK

Take a few moments to complete Worksheet #8: Designing An Outcomes-Based Performance Improvement Project, which is on pages 153–155 in the Appendix. Think of a performance improvement project you would like to recommend or one that is just beginning. Use the worksheet to document all the critical issues related to this improvement opportunity. Search out the answers to those questions you are unable to answer immediately. You may also find it helpful to complete this worksheet at the outset of a performance measurement and improvement project.

Data Management

When initiating and conducting an outcomes-oriented performance measurement and improvement project, keep in mind the key relationships among knowledge, information, measures, and data. Data are facts collected to calculate a measure. Measures are combinations of data elements. When measures are analyzed, understood, and interpreted they become information. Using information to improve performance generates knowledge. Figure 5-1, page 76, graphically illustrates these concepts.

Data management, which includes a number of discrete activities, is a major process component of every outcomes-based improvement project. Improvement team members will invest significant time, thought, and energy into preparing for collecting data, analyzing data, generating improvement ideas, and reporting findings. Figure 5-2, page 77, presents a flowchart of a data management process that an improvement team might implement.

THOUGHT BREAK

■ *How would you define data management?*

■ *What are the usual components of data management at your organization?*

■ *How are these activities implemented?*

■ *How useful and meaningful are each of these steps?*

Prepare for Data Collection

Preparing for the collection of key performance data is an important subprocess of the data management process. It involves the

■ specification of information and data needs, in relation to the specific goals of the improvement project;

■ specification of indicators;

■ definition of data elements;

■ documentation of the data collection plan (such as sample, collection times/frequencies, data collectors, data collection training, and so on);

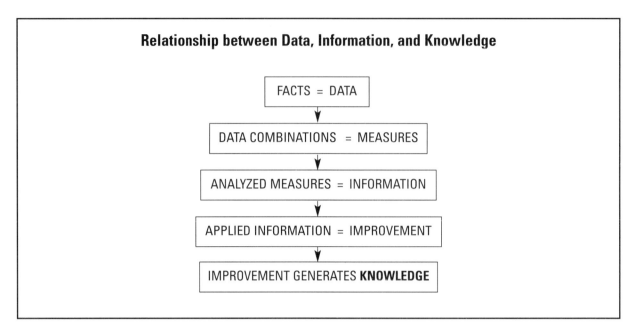

Figure 5-1. *This figure shows the interconnected relationships between data, measures, information, improvement, and knowledge.*

- specification of data sources;
- creation of the data collection instrument;
- determination of appropriate data analysis strategies;
- pilot testing the collection and analysis of data; and
- modification of the data collection and analysis approaches, based on the pilot test findings.

Review the specific purpose(s) of your outcomes-focused improvement project and determine what information, measures, and data are necessary to achieve those purposes. Refer to the completed project design document(Worksheet #8) when your team is brainstorming project knowledge, information, and data needs. First, describe the knowledge about improvement in performance that you strive to gain. Next, identify the information that will generate that knowledge. Then, determine what specific measures and data are essential for the production of necessary information. At this point, create a comprehensive list of the needed data.

Review the information your team needs, specify performance measures that will generate that information, and identify the data that compose these measures. Depending on your data needs, your team may adopt or adapt measures that

- are being used in other projects at your organization or health care system;
- have been described in the professional literature;
- are available through professional associations; and
- are promulgated by proprietary organizations.

You will often be able to use existing measures. You may find the need, however, to develop "custom" measures, designed exclusively with your specific information needs in mind. If or when that occurs, your team should take responsibility for specifying the data needed to calculate each specific measure.

Define any indicator data elements. As explained in *The Measurement Mandate*, indicators are composed of data elements that define the indicator's generality or precision. Since they often reflect patient demographics and characteristics, they may also provide risk adjustment data. Typically, data elements are discrete pieces of data, such as birth dates, times, principal diagnoses, and discrete, descriptive clinical or other facts that can be quantified.[1]

The following are two examples of an indicator and its data elements that relate to an ambulatory care organization:

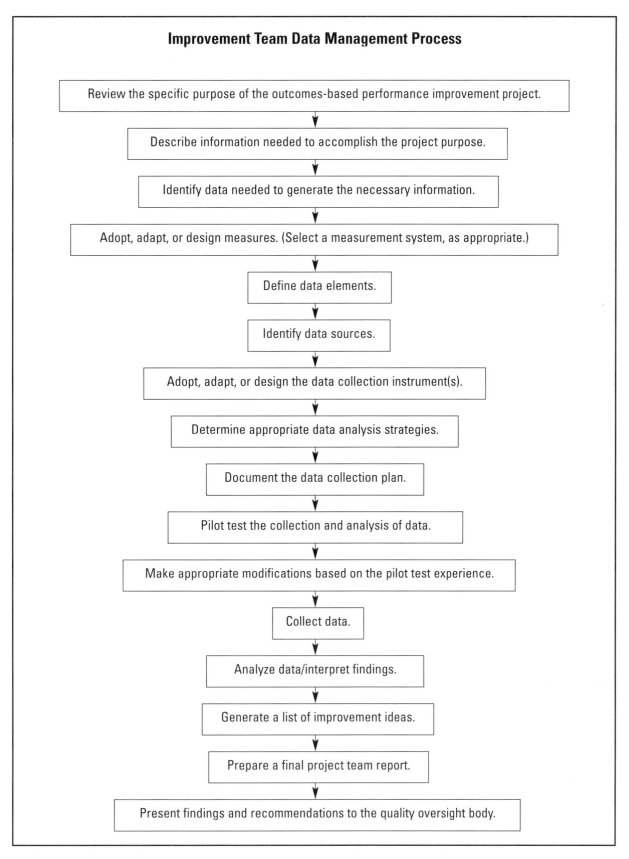

Figure 5-2. *This flowchart illustrates one way an improvement team might implement a data management process.*

INDICATOR:
Monthly percentage of the total number of patients in each of the following age categories: children (0–12.11 years), adolescents (13–21.11 years), adults (22–65.11 years), and older adults (older than 65 years) who are referred to hospital-based emergency departments from the urgent care center.

DATA ELEMENTS:
1. Patient's birth date   mm/dd/yy
2. Referred to the emergency
    department   yes   no

INDICATOR:
Monthly percentage of the total number of patients seen in the correctional health center that are treated by nurse practitioners (NP), physician assistants (PA), and physicians (MD).

DATA ELEMENTS:
1. Total number of patients seen _____
2. Number of patients treated by:
    NP _____
    PA _____
    MD _____

THOUGHT BREAK

■ *Review how you determine what indicators are necessary for a specific measurement initiative.*

■ *What are the sources of these indicators?*

■ *How do you describe/define the indicators so that data are collected accurately and consistently?*

Once the measures are identified and the data elements defined, it is possible to identify the sources for all needed data. Performance data may be extracted from many sources. First, consider the nature of the data your team requires. It may be clinical, operational, administrative, financial, or satisfaction-based. It may reflect processes or outcomes. It is probably quantitative, but may be qualitative. Then, consider where to logically find such data.

The patient record is a rich source of clinical process and outcomes data. Often admission packets, assessment tools, problem lists, treatment plans, flowsheets, and chart notes provide required clinical outcomes data. Frequently, internal management reports present useful clinical data, such as patient demographics, case mix, reasons for visits, and frequency of visits. Infection control and diagnostic reports are also sometimes a source of needed clinical data.

Operational, administrative, and financial data may also be abstracted from routine internal management reports. These reports typically include data on numbers and mix of staff, staff competency, and absenteeism. Administrative reports often present useful data about numbers of patients seen, numbers/types of diagnostic work-ups, referral sources, and patient disposition. Incident and risk management reports offer detailed data about sentinel events—those occurrences that jeopardize the physical or psychological health, well-being, and/or safety of patients. Liability claims data may be helpful, but are often difficult to access because of confidentiality concerns. Financial reports include important data about payer sources, reimbursement rates, costs of care for a spectrum of diagnoses and services, and expense/revenue ratios.

Satisfaction surveys, as the name suggests, often provide needed data describing patients' and staff's degree of satisfaction with the organization and its services. Market research reports may offer interesting data about community and patient service needs.

As you explore the spectrum of possible data sources, document the actual data sources or locations that you discover. Such information will be helpful to include on data collection tools. In addition, the straightforward documentation of data sources will be an especially helpful reference when, at the conclusion of the improvement project, the improvement team disbands and the ongoing data collection is assigned, as a routine part of an individual's or entity's daily work.

Data collection instruments consist of indicators and data elements and facilitate the consistent acquisition of performance data. As was true with your search for indicators, diligent exploration may lead to the discovery of extant data collection tools that your improvement team could adopt. However, you are more likely to find data collection tools that your team can use, with modifications. You may also be challenged to design a new data collection instrument. Doing so requires a bit of forethought and much attention to detail.

Remember, your selected measures and defined data elements are the main components of a data collection instrument. In addition to that information, the tool should include sections for documenting the date and time of data collection, the name of the data collector, the data source for each indicator and defined data element, general data collection instructions, any pertinent sampling instructions, and any other important miscellaneous information. You will pilot test the data collection instrument to assess and ensure its usability. Such a pilot guarantees your team at least one more planned opportunity to revise the data collection tool.

THOUGHT BREAK

■ *Consider how data collection instruments are acquired, revised, or developed at your organization.*

■ *Do you look for existing data collection tools? Or, do you routinely create new tools?*

■ *Where do you or might you look for existing tools?*

■ *How do you determine whether to use an available data collection tool "as is" or with modifications?*

■ *If you must generate a new tool, who is involved in the creation of the instrument? Who helps to design it and who reviews it?*

■ *Is each data collection tool approved? If so, by whom?*

In order to determine the most effective data analysis strategies, the improvement team must carefully consider the type of data that will be collected and how it will be used to improve performance. The data analysis techniques applied in an outcomes-based performance improvement project derive directly from the specific goals of the improvement effort and the type of data that are collected. The type of data collected is driven by

the project-specific information needs. There are two fundamental kinds of studies: quantitative and qualitative. Each is associated with a particular type of information need, data collection approach, and data analysis strategy.

Quantitative studies use structured techniques to objectively understand traits and characteristics, as well as the relationship between or among variables of interest. These data are objective, discrete, and readily measurable. Quantitative data are submitted to a variety of statistical procedures that can describe performance, reveal correlations among variables, calculate process capability, and identify the type of variation that is present. Quantitative data are reported as rates, ratios, percents, averages, standard deviations, correlation coefficients, data runs, control limits, and specification limits or performance tolerances.

Qualitative studies employ direct observation and interviews to unearth human feelings, perceptions, values, beliefs, meanings, and thoughts. Through painstaking documentation and intensive analysis, the gestalt of the human experience is exposed and described. Qualitative data are narrative, descriptive, expressive, detailed, and rich. Analysis of qualitative data seeks to illustrate the complex themes and patterns of human experiences. These data are reported as direct quotations, paraphrased descriptions, and summaries of predominant and recurring themes.

Outcomes-based performance measurement and improvement can exploit the strengths of both quantitative and qualitative methods. For example, a variety of closed-ended surveys may be used to track changes in patient symptoms and functionality (quantitative), and a few open-ended questions may be asked to uncover the patients' subjective experiences of well-being (qualitative).

Both study methods have advantages and disadvantages. Quantitative studies are generally fairly easy and inexpensive to implement. They are very useful for presenting general performance information. They cannot, however, capture subjective human experiences in compelling descriptive detail. Qualitative studies are often costly and time-consuming. They are immensely helpful, though, in providing intense, detail-rich, personal descriptions. As such, they are beneficial in understanding the needs, expectations, and experiences of patients and other key stakeholders.

THOUGHT BREAK

■ *Think about the performance measurement initiatives at your organization.*

■ *Do they tend to be quantitative, qualitative, or both?*

■ *How are quantitative data typically collected and analyzed?*

■ *How are qualitative data usually collected and analyzed?*

A data collection plan is a written document that is used to operationalize the measurement component(s) of a performance improvement project. Several key pieces of information are provided in the data collection plan. A short (one or two-sentence) description of the measurement/improvement project is presented. The population of interest is specified and the sampling strategy is described. Any limitations or constraints as a result of sampling are documented. It is beneficial to use true random, stratified random, or stratified samples to the greatest extent possible. Such samples allow for broader generalizations of findings. An inability to use such samples should not prohibit performance measurement and improvement activities. Convenience samples are often used for performance measurement activities. Such samples are acceptable. However, be cautious about widely generalizing the findings from a study conducted with convenience samples. The sources of data are identified and described, if necessary. A synopsis of any data collection training is included. A brief description of the data collectors is also provided. Finally, the project time line, emphasizing data management activities, is presented.

As you draft the data collection plan, think about the data collection resource load attached to your improvement project. Recall how common it is for organizations to engage in multiple data collection activities simultaneously. Investigate what data collection instruments and measurement systems are currently in use throughout your organization. Talk with colleagues and coworkers to determine if the data required by your team are already being collected elsewhere in the organization. If so, create a "data-sharing agreement," so that one team or individual collects data for multiple users and purposes. Such a partnership reduces your organization's data collection burden by minimizing duplicative data collection efforts. At the same time, it frees resources for other aspects of the improvement effort.

EXERCISE BREAK

Take a few moments to complete Worksheet #9: Data Management Plan, which is on pages 156–158 in the Appendix. Think of the same performance improvement project you thought about when completing Worksheet #8. Use this worksheet to document all the critical data management issues related to this improvement opportunity. Part I of the worksheet will help you prepare for data collection. Part II will help you prepare for data analysis. Part III is a form for documenting your plans for data collection and analysis. Part IV is a data management time line, on which you can indicate your projected and actual completion dates for critical activities. You may also find it helpful to complete this worksheet at the outset of a performance measurement and improvement project.

The final steps left in the subprocess of preparing for data collection are to pilot the data collection tool and analysis strategies and make modifications in either or both, depending on the results of the pilot test. A pilot test is, fundamentally, a controlled simulation of the data collection and analysis subprocesses. The purpose of the pilot test is to uncover any problems or weaknesses with the data collection tool, data collection process, data analysis strategy, or data display formats. A pilot test is conducted with a very small sample. Often, no more than ten cases are included.

The pilot test may demonstrate the need to edit the data collection tool, modify the data collection process, revise the data analysis strategy, and/or change data display formats. Unless such changes are very minor, a second pilot should be conducted to test the effect of the changes and modifications. The performance measurement processes of an improvement project generally do not require more than two pilots.

THOUGHT BREAK

■ *When conducting performance measurement in your organization, are data collection and analysis approaches routinely pilot tested?*

■ *If so, how is the pilot conducted?*

■ *If not, why not?*

■ *How can pilot tests be conducted in your organization without unnecessarily burdening, complicating, or lengthening the measurement initiatives?*

Collect Data

The successful collection of data becomes a fairly simple process, provided it follows a thorough, organized preparation for data acquisition. Maintaining data integrity is a quality control function that should be operative throughout the data collection period. Such a function ensures that

■ data confidentiality and security are maintained;

■ data collection instruments are used correctly;

■ all needed data are abstracted and entered on the data collection form; and

■ no critical data are missing.

To avoid compromising data integrity, document clinical data during or immediately following a patient visit. This instruction must be communicated clearly to staff who will serve as data collectors.

For analysis purposes, collected data must become a part of a performance database. This database may or may not be computerized. Some data collection strategies (such as data entry into a laptop or notebook computer)

enable abstracted data to be entered directly into the database. If your data collection process does not, the additional step of transferring information from the data collection tool into the database must be implemented. It is usually possible to perform this data entry task with the data that have already been collected, while data collectors continue to acquire additional data, in accordance with your data collection plan.

Analyze and Interpret Data

As you were designing your improvement project and preparing for data collection, you decided how to analyze the performance data that your team would generate. Most likely, you will be using quantitative analysis methods. Once you have collected all the desired data, you should begin analyzing, displaying and interpreting the data.

Performance improvement data analysis is squarely focused on understanding current performance and the causes for current performance. Statistics, such as measures of central tendency, standard deviation, t-tests, chi square, ANOVA, log linear regression, factor analysis, and process capability and variation may be applied to aggregated data to understand process operations, performance outcomes, and the relationship between processes and outcomes. Analyses will present information about

■ average outcomes achieved;

■ outcomes occurrence rates;

■ outcomes achieved over time;

■ variability of outcomes;

■ the relationship between outcomes and other key variables such as gender, age, diagnosis, symptoms, and so on; and

■ the relationship between outcomes and processes.

Improvement-focused data analysis also includes comparative analyses of two types. First, an organization examines its own performance over time. Data may be examined and displayed in "rolling" 12 or 18-month periods. For example, your physical therapy agency might track the number of physical therapy visits and length of time it takes for workers' compensation patients with low back pain to return to work. Alternatively, your primary care center may monitor the percentage of patient population seeking obstetric, pediatric, internal medicine, and family practice services. Your freestanding military clinic may log the percentage of patients seen that are active military personnel, their beneficiaries, retired military personnel, and their beneficiaries. This rolling data presentation facilitates a quick and relatively simple understanding of the ongoing, continuous performance of the organization. Often, such time series data are displayed on run charts or control charts. Both demonstrate performance levels and illustrate the variation in the processes or outcomes of interest. Using control charts helps identify of the type of variation (common cause or special cause) present in the performance system. The development of effective improvement strategies is ultimately dependent on this understanding of performance variation.

Sometimes performance data for a particular quarter of the year are compared to performance data for the same quarter during previous years. Financial, administrative, and critical incident data are often examined and presented this way. For instance, your Medicare-certified ambulatory surgery center may compare expense/revenue ratios for the second quarter of the current year to the second quarter of the preceding three years. Your Veteran's Affairs clinics may compare the number of patients seen, by number of visits (one, two-three, or more than three), for the first quarter of the current year to the first quarter of the previous two years. Your birthing center may compare average number of births for the fourth quarter of the current year to the fourth quarter of the prior five years. This type of comparative data is generally presented in a table or line or bar graph format. It is important to note that this quarter-to-quarter analysis has a significant limitation. It fails to present a continuous picture of longitudinal performance. It is, therefore, of only limited value in helping organizations to understand ongoing performance and track continuous improvement in an uninterrupted fashion.

The second type of improvement-focused comparative analysis is benchmarking. Benchmarking

is accurately defined in multiple ways, according to organization consultant Michael J. Spendolini, PhD. All definitions agree that benchmarking is a goal-directed process. Thereafter, the differing definitions variously describe and emphasize different aspects of the process. The following definition of benchmarking was constructed from Dr. Spendolini's benchmarking menu and is applicable to this discussion:

> Benchmarking is a continuous, systematic, organized process for improving the performance of the ambulatory care organization by comparing selected services and functions to those of other organizations that are identified as representing best practices.[2]

Once an ambulatory care organization has measured and discovered its performance, it can examine its services, processes, and/or outcomes in relation to

- comparative performance databases, which may be at a national, regional, or health system level;
- professionally recognized standards of practice and care;
- "best practices" organizations; and/or
- competitors.

For example, your primary care center may compare the outcomes of your patients, age 14 and older, suffering from rheumatoid arthritis with those developed by the Health Outcomes Institute. Alternatively, your birthing center may compare the percentage of women with live births who received prenatal care in the first trimester of pregnancy with the comparative prenatal care data captured in the Health Plan Employer Data and Information Set (HEDIS). Your independent practitioner practice may compare patient satisfaction with appointment wait times for serious problems and well care visits to member satisfaction with access/wait times assessed by Kaiser Permanente of Northern California.

THOUGHT BREAK

- *Consider comparative performance data analysis techniques.*

- *How does your organization examine and evaluate its own performance over time?*

- *Do you compare your organization's performance with that of exemplary organizations, established databases, accepted practice standards, and/or published guidelines?*

- *If not, why not?*

- *How can comparative analysis of your organization's performance be strengthened?*

Root cause analysis is an intensive process of searching out and identifying the causes of performance. Root cause analysis is not a single tool or technique. Rather, it is an approach for explicating the causes of performance outcomes. It employs a variety of tools that help foster an understanding of how key processes work and how such processes lead to outcomes.

The following discussion explores five tools frequently used to facilitate a comprehensive root cause analysis: cause-effect diagram, Pareto analysis/chart, process flow diagram, Repetitive Why?, and scatter diagram. A brief explanation of each tool is provided.

Cause–Effect Diagram

The cause–effect diagram is a specialized form of brainstorming that facilitates the discovery of specific causes for a defined result. The cause–effect diagram generally illuminates four domains of performance etiologies:

- Human factors, which include staff knowledge, skills, attitudes, feelings, staffing levels, patient condition, patient ability to learn care techniques, social support systems, and so on;

- Methods factors, which represent the fundamental ways in which services are delivered, include policies, procedures, practices, protocols, and treatment approaches;

- Materials factors, which are non-machine/non-electronic items used in the provision of services, include practice standards, critical pathways, patient education material, medications, syringes, ophthalmoscopes, and gurneys, and so on; and

- Machines, which are electronic devices used to directly or indirectly support service provision, include IV pumps and controllers, cardiac monitors, pulse oximeters, endoscopes, CT scanners, and MRIs, and so on.

A typical cause–effect diagram will have many causes associated with one or two factors and fewer causes associated with remaining factors. The distribution of causes helps to highlight areas for possible significant improvement.

Pareto Analysis/Chart

Pareto analysis is based on the theory that a few critical causes make the greatest contribution to an effect. The "80/20 Rule," which states that 80% of effects result from 20% of causes, is commonly used to explain Pareto Analysis. The 20% of causes that lead to 80% of results are known as the "vital few": the small number of causes that account for the greatest number of effects. The remaining 80% of causes are known as the "trivial many": those multiple reasons for a small number of effects. The Pareto chart, which is a specialized bar graph, is a useful tool for root cause analysis because it helps to identify the proportional contribution that different causative factors make to an outcome. Bar graphs visually illustrate, in descending order from left to right, those items that contribute most heavily to an effect. Frequently, a Pareto chart includes a line graph that illustrates the cumulative percentage of contribution to the effect made by the different causes. By identifying degrees of contribution to an outcome it offers direction about where to dedicate resources—to the vital few—for maximal impact. For example, a Pareto chart may show that preoperative counseling, patient support, accessibility of the surgeon, postoperative pain management, preoperative patient teaching, and postoperative teaching, in that order, increase the likelihood of patient satisfaction with plastic surgery.

Process Flow Diagram

The process flow diagram is a useful root cause analysis tool. It is traditionally used to create a detailed picture of how the targeted process actually operates. It may also be used to draft and assess a revised or new process when a project team is focused on making actual improvements. Sometimes the simple act of drawing the process picture begins to identify vulnerable or problematic areas that contribute to the achieved outcomes. In-depth process analysis examines the overall process and each process step for effectiveness and efficiency. It also involves an analysis of the total process for unrestricted work flow, smooth transitions or "handoffs," and appropriate directionality. Process analysis tries to diagnose malfunctioning processes by looking for purposeless actions, redundancy, areas of unknown activity, unnecessary action steps, inconsistency, and frequent or common obstacles. The overall goal of an in-depth process analysis is to identify high impact areas for improvement by determining critical process weaknesses or problems.

Repetitive Why?

Root cause analysis is also characterized by the repetitive asking of the simple question: Why? By probing for more specific answers, you can dig deeply for causes and avoid mistakenly interpreting an effect as a cause. When the question Why? fails to produce a new answer, you have likely identified at least one of the root causes of the performance.

Scatter Diagram

The scatter diagram facilitates a root cause analysis by illustrating the relationship between two variables of interest. Although it cannot demonstrate causality, a scatter diagram can show correlation. For this reason, it is especially helpful when testing a theory about the impact one variable or factor has on another variable or factor. A scatter diagram can illustrate several possible relationship patterns between two variables. It may demonstrate a positive correlation, which means as one variable changes, the other variable changes in the same way. For example, the risk of infection in a patient receiving outpatient cancer chemotherapy increases as her/his public exposure to large numbers of people increases. A scatter diagram may illustrate a negative relationship between two variables. This

means that as one variable changes, the other variable changes in an opposing manner. For example, the risk of infection in a patient receiving outpatient cancer chemotherapy increases as white blood count decreases. Finally, a scatter diagram may show that two variables are not related in any clearly observable way. For example, the risk of infection in a patient receiving outpatient cancer chemotherapy increases as blood pressure elevates.

An Example of a Root Cause Analysis

While reviewing utilization data for the past 12 months, an ambulatory surgery center (ASC) notices that 25% (100) of the 400 pediatric patients that had undergone tonsillectomy and adenoidectomy (T & A) visited the emergency department less than 24 hours after the surgery.

Although they do not know the cause, the ASC staff are concerned about this outcome. Once the staff are committed to understanding why this occurred and how they can reduce the number of emergency room visits, they conduct a root cause analysis.

First, the staff needs to understand the pediatric T & A process, from the time when the decision to operate is made through the follow-up postoperative call. Therefore, they begin the root cause analysis by creating the "high level" process flow diagram of the T & A process, as demonstrated in Figure 5-3, pages 85–86.

Once they have a clearer picture of the T & A process, the staff wonders why parents returned to the emergency room and what resulted from the emergency clinical evaluation. Thus, they review the records of all 100 children brought to the emergency room. They document the parents' stated reason(s) for bringing their child to the emergency department, the emergency physician's assessment of the child's condition, and the disposition of the child. As illustrated in the Pareto chart in Figure 5-4, page 87, data analysis identified five main reasons for emergency room visits. In no instance was a child's clinical status documented as unstable or were post-T & A complications noted. None of these patients was admitted. All children were discharged to home after the

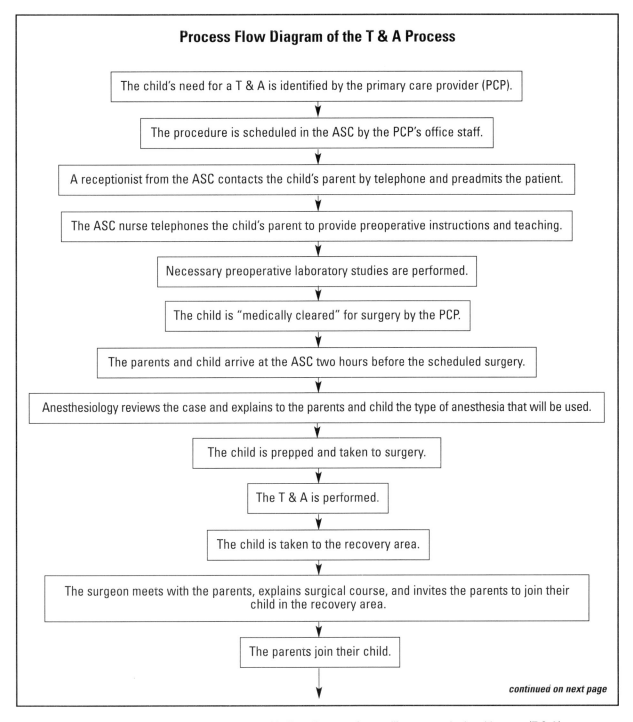

Figure 5-3. *Staff at an ambulatory surgery center use this flow diagram of a tonsillectomy and adenoidectomy (T & A) process to determine why pediatric patients visited an emergency department postoperatively.*

parents received focused teaching about what to expect during the next 48–72 hours after the surgery.

Now that the ASC staff understands what symptoms caused these 100 parents to feel an

emergency medical evaluation was necessary, the staff begins to wonder why this group of parents (unlike the 75% who did not visit the emergency department unnecessarily) misinterpreted the significance of their child's symptoms or misunderstood how to best respond to

Inside the figure:

Process Flow Diagram of the T & A Process

The child's need for a T & A is identified by the primary care provider (PCP).

The procedure is scheduled in the ASC by the PCP's office staff.

A receptionist from the ASC contacts the child's parent by telephone and preadmits the patient.

The ASC nurse telephones the child's parent to provide preoperative instructions and teaching.

Necessary preoperative laboratory studies are performed.

The child is "medically cleared" for surgery by the PCP.

The parents and child arrive at the ASC two hours before the scheduled surgery.

Anesthesiology reviews the case and explains to the parents and child the type of anesthesia that will be used.

The child is prepped and taken to surgery.

The T & A is performed.

The child is taken to the recovery area.

The surgeon meets with the parents, explains surgical course, and invites the parents to join their child in the recovery area.

The parents join their child.

continued on next page

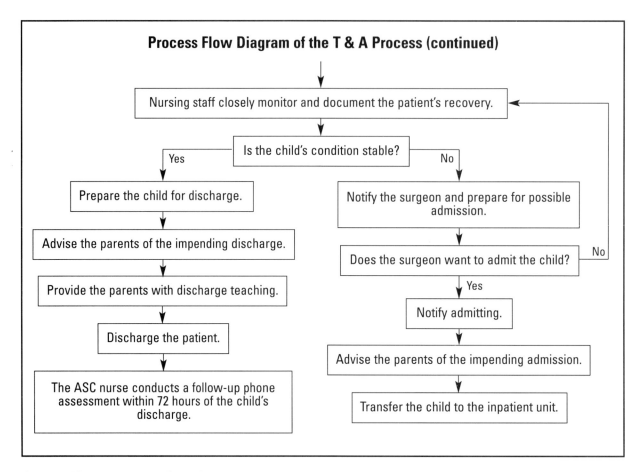

Process Flow Diagram of the T & A Process (continued)

Nursing staff closely monitor and document the patient's recovery.

Is the child's condition stable?

Yes

Prepare the child for discharge.

Advise the parents of the impending discharge.

Provide the parents with discharge teaching.

Discharge the patient.

The ASC nurse conducts a follow-up phone assessment within 72 hours of the child's discharge.

No

Notify the surgeon and prepare for possible admission.

Does the surgeon want to admit the child?

No

Yes

Notify admitting.

Advise the parents of the impending admission.

Transfer the child to the inpatient unit.

the specific symptoms. Thus, they use a cause-effect diagram (see Figure 5-5, page 88) to brainstorm significant possible causes of parent misunderstanding in the five main symptoms revealed in the Pareto analysis.

Although the ASC staff has now identified possible causes for parental misunderstanding of symptoms, they are very interested in speaking directly with some of the parents who had taken their children to the emergency room. They want to query them specifically about why they made the emergency room decision. After examining current workload, they determine that they can reasonably talk with 25–30 parents. Ultimately, they are able to engage 24 of the 30 parents they telephone.

By using the Repetitive Why? technique, staff discover the following likely root cause for misinterpreting the meaning of their child's symptoms. Figure 5-6, pages 89–90, shows the Repetitive Why? technique in more detail.

Parental lack of understanding of normal postoperative symptoms and course of recovery occurred because of the following:

1. Ineffective patient education:
   a. Inadequate time for patient teaching and learning,
   b. Inadequate patient teaching approaches,
   c. Inadequate patient teaching/learning/support tools,
   d. Failure to validate learning, and
   e. Communication barriers (language and words); and
2. Fear, anxiety, worry, and nervousness about their child's condition and their own ability to properly care for the child at home.

Seventy-five percent (300) of the 400 parents of children who had T & A procedures during the past year, did not bring their child unnecessarily to the emergency room postoperatively. This majority of parents had no apparent difficulties understanding what to expect in the immediate

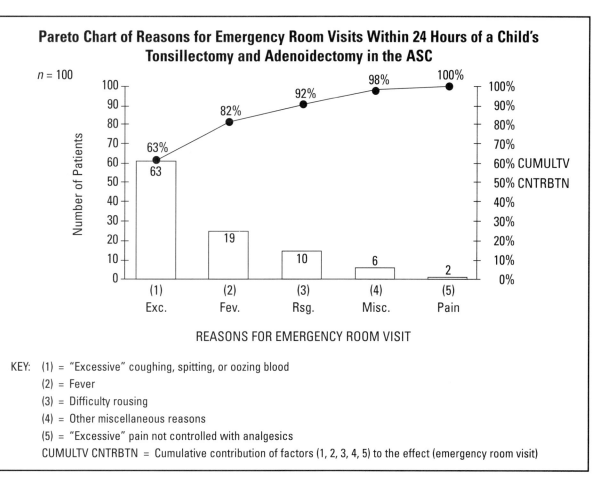

Figure 5-4. *This Pareto chart identifies the five main reasons for postoperative emergency visits.*

postoperative period or what to do based on what they observed.

But a large subset of parents (25%) did seem to have trouble understanding what to expect in the 24 hours immediately following their child's T & A surgery. They were unclear about how to deal with the different postoperative symptoms their child experienced. They were not sure when it was necessary to seek professional assistance.

Staff ask, "What differentiates the 75% of parents from the 25% of parents?" They review what they have learned thus far:

1. Preparing parents to actively engage in the care of their child occurs near the end of the T & A process—when patient discharge teaching is provided.

2. Four major symptoms caused 100 parents (25% of the total parent population) to bring their children to the emergency room

postoperatively. Sixty-three percent of these 100 parents came to the emergency room for the same single symptom: "excessive" coughing, spitting, or oozing blood.

3. Approaches to parent teaching (methods factors) and characteristics and abilities of the parents and staff providing the teaching (human factors) appear to contribute heavily to parental misinterpretation of the significance of their child's postoperative symptoms.

4. Parents who return their child to the emergency room within 24 hours of discharge from the ASC appear to do so primarily because they are uncertain about the meaning of their child's symptoms/complaints and how they, themselves, should manage these symptoms/complaints.

The ASC staff ask themselves again, "What differentiates the 75% of parents from the 25% of

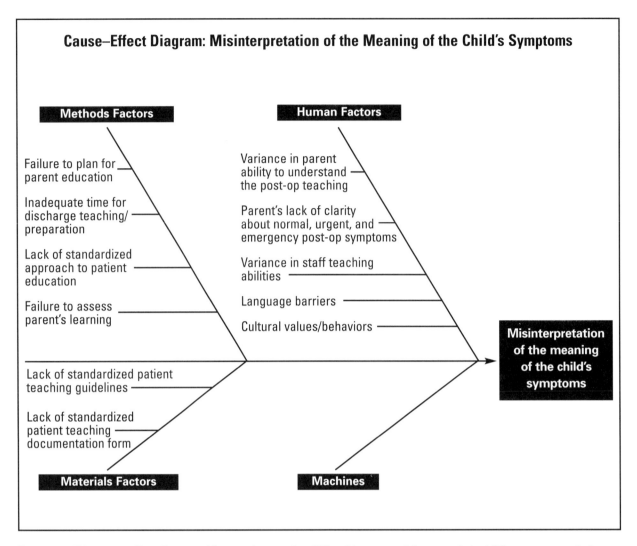

Figure 5-5. *This cause–effect diagram addresses the question, "Why did parents misinterpret their child's symptoms as indicators of the need for emergency treatment?"*

parents?" They generate a theory, based on what they have learned, to answer this pivotal question. Their theory is:

> Parents who are confident in their own abilities to care for their child during those first 24 hours after a tonsillectomy and adenoidectomy do not bring their recovering child to the emergency room unnecessarily.

The reciprocal theory is:

> Parents who lack confidence in their own abilities to care for their child during those first 24 hours after a tonsillectomy and adenoidectomy bring their recovering child to the emergency room unnecessarily for evaluation of symptoms that do not warrant an emergency assessment.

If the theory about parent confidence is true, staff will need to explore ways of maximizing parental confidence. But first, they need to test the theory. They decide to do so by conducting a one-question telephone survey with a stratified random sample drawn from the population of parents whose children underwent a T & A in the previous 12 months. The stratification is parents who did and did not bring their child to the emergency department during the first 24 hours post-T & A. Thirty-five parents are randomly selected from each of the two groups. A total of 59 parents (32 who did/27 who did not bring their child to the emergency room) agree to participate in the phone survey.

The Repetitive Why?: Exploring Why Parents Misinterpreted the Meaning of Their Child's Post-T & A Symptoms

Q: "Why did you take your child to the emergency room after surgery?"

A: "Because I was worried that something was wrong."

Q: "Why were you worried that something was wrong?"

(Please note that these answers clustered into several response categories that correspond with the Pareto categories staff developed after reviewing information documented in the patient records.)

A: #1: "Because there was so much blood. It never stopped."

#2: "Because s/he had a fever that didn't go away, even after I gave the acetaminophen the doctor prescribed."

#3: "Because all s/he did was sleep. S/he couldn't stay awake. And it was very difficult for me to wake him/her up."

#4: "Because s/he kept crying and telling me that his/her throat hurt so bad; that the pain medicine didn't help the sore throat at all."

Q: "Why did you think this symptom meant something was wrong?"

A: "Because I didn't know what was supposed to happen; how s/he should feel. I didn't know what was normal and what was a problem."

Q: "Why didn't you know what was supposed to happen? What was normal?"

A: "Because they didn't explain it to me very well."

Q: "Why didn't they explain it very well?"

A: "Because the doctors and nurses are so busy, they're always rushing. They just didn't have enough time."

Q: "Why didn't they have enough time?"

A: "I don't know. They're just too busy."

Q: "Why didn't you know what was supposed to happen? What was normal? What are some other reasons?"

A: "Because I didn't really understand what they did tell me."

Q: "Why didn't you understand what they did tell you?"

(Please note the two related but different responses to this query.)

A: #1: "Because they explained it in ways I couldn't understand; using medical words."

#2: "Because English is not my first language; sometimes I have a hard time understanding things. Like what certain words or sentences mean, exactly, especially if they're complicated."

Q: "Why did they use words you don't understand; medical words? A language that you have difficulty understanding?"

A: "Because that's how doctors and nurses talk. They forget that patients don't always know what they mean. They think everyone is familiar with medical terms. They expect everyone to know English as well as they do. But not everyone does."

Q: "Why didn't the doctors and nurses know you didn't understand what they told you?"

A: "Because they never asked me if I understood what they told me."

Q: "Why didn't they ask you if you understood what they told you?"

A: "I don't know. They just didn't. Maybe they assumed I automatically understood what they meant. I don't know. They didn't ask me."

continued on next page

Figure 5-6. *The use of the Repetitive Why? technique shows how staff discovered the root cause of parents misinterpreting their child's symptoms.*

The Repetitive Why?: Exploring Why Parents Misinterpreted the Meaning of Their Child's Post-T & A Symptoms (continued)

Q: "Why didn't the doctors and nurses know you didn't understand what they told you? What are some other reasons?"

A: "Because I didn't tell them I didn't understand their explanations."

Q: "Why didn't you tell them you didn't understand their explanations?"

A: "Because I didn't want to take up any more of their time—they're so busy. Plus, I didn't want them to think I was stupid and unable to take care of my son/daughter."

Q: "Why didn't you understand what they did tell you? What are some other reasons?"

A: "Because they told me all this stuff about bleeding and that s/he would have a pretty bad sore throat and maybe some trouble swallowing. They told me I should keep his/her head up on a pillow and put ice on his/her throat and to make her/him eat lots of popsicles so that s/he wouldn't get dehydrated. They reminded me several times that if s/he wasn't getting better, if there was a lot of bleeding, or the pain was really severe, or s/he developed a high fever, I should come to the hospital right away. So, that's what I did. I came to the emergency room. I just couldn't remember; I just didn't know if what was happening was normal."

Q: "Why couldn't you remember what was normal and what wasn't normal?"

A: "Because there was so much to keep straight in my head. And I was worried about my son/daughter. I just couldn't keep it all clear in my mind."

Q: "Why did you have to keep it all clear in your mind?"

A: "Because I'm responsible for my child."

Q: "Why did you have to keep all the information the doctors and nurses gave you in your head instead of someplace else?"

A: "Because they just told me what they wanted me to know. They didn't really give me anything to help me understand or remember what they told me."

Q: "Why didn't they give you anything to help you understand and remember what they told you?"

A: "I don't know. They did give me one sheet of paper to take with me. But, it wasn't too helpful. It reminded me to call the doctor to set up an appointment for my daughter/son. Well, that I can remember; that's not hard. It also had some information about what medicine I should give him/her. I guess that was helpful. And it listed a number of things that were reasons to call the doctor or go to the hospital. Things like a lot of bleeding, or swelling around the throat, or if s/he couldn't swallow liquid, or a high fever developed, or if the pain was really bad and the medicine didn't relieve it. The list was pretty scary, actually. I think it scared me more than it helped me."

Q: "Why did the sheet they gave you scare you? Why didn't it help you understand and remember what they told you?"

A: "I don't know. Everything just sounded so serious and dangerous. It just didn't tell me what I needed to know. It didn't help me know what to do. Well, maybe it did say the right things to do. But, I couldn't really understand them. So, I didn't know what I should do and the sheet made it sound so risky not to go to the hospital. It seemed like going to the emergency room was the best, the safest thing to do. And, they didn't really explain the information on the sheet when they gave it to me, either. They handed it to me and said here's what you should watch out for. They reminded me to make an appointment with the doctor. And that was it. I was sort of on my own. So, it really didn't help me remember or better understand what I had to do to take care of my daughter/son. I guess I decided before we even left the surgery center that if something didn't seem right I would just turn around and come right back to the hospital. "

Q: "Why didn't they explain the information on the sheet when they gave it to you?"

A: "I don't know."

Q: "Why didn't you understand what they did tell you? What are some other reasons?"

A: "I don't know. Maybe there aren't any other reasons. Maybe it's just what I already said. They didn't find out if I knew what their explanations meant. They didn't have enough time to spend with me. They didn't have written explanations or instructions that were detailed enough. That's why I didn't understand. Plus, I was nervous and worried about my child. It was hard for me to concentrate. I think those are all the reasons I didn't understand what would normally happen after this surgery."

The ASC staff ask each parent the same question:

> "Recall when your child had the T & A surgery. When you were leaving the ASC, how confident did you feel about your ability to take care of your child during the first 24 hours after surgery?"

____ VERY CONFIDENT	____ CONFIDENT
____ NOT VERY CONFIDENT	____ NOT CONFIDENT AT ALL

They use their data to plot the scatter diagram in Figure 5-7, page 92.

The scatter diagram in Figure 5-7 shows the relationship the ASC staff think it will. It does, in fact, seem to be true that some type of inverse relationship exists between parental confidence and return to the emergency department with their child in the first 24 hours post-T & A.

With this growing understanding of the possible root causes of this undesirable outcome, staff at the ASC are ready to begin thinking about improvement ideas.

For information about other performance improvement tools specific for ambulatory care, refer to the Joint Commission's *Using Performance Improvement Tools in Ambulatory Care.*

THOUGHT BREAK

■ *Is systematic root cause analysis a standard part of all your organization's performance measurement and improvement initiatives?*

■ *If so, how do you conduct root cause analysis?*

■ *What tools do your teams use?*

■ *If root cause analysis is not a standard part, why not?*

■ *What must be done for improvement teams at your organization to routinely conduct root cause analysis as a part of assessment of performance?*

Enumerate Improvement Ideas

All the project team's activities lead to this climax: the generation of improvement ideas. By analyzing pertinent performance data, studying process operations, determining root causes, and clarifying the vital few causes for the major outcomes, the improvement team has come a long way in understanding how and why the current outcomes are being achieved.

What can now occur as the product of this intense analysis is the generative component of the performance improvement process. At this point, the improvement team is well positioned to propose a series of focused, fact-based recommendations about how to improve performance. With a rich appreciation of what factors contribute, in what ways and to what outcomes, the improvement team can recommend process modifications, the design of new processes, the delivery of new services, the forging of new partnerships, and the building of new bridges within and outside the organization. Improvement suggestions can foster consistent achievement of better outcomes, heighten patient satisfaction with services and their health care experience, improve the effectiveness of services, improve the efficiency of operations, reduce expense, possibly generate new revenue, and boost staff morale and satisfaction with the work experience.

At this point a fatigued project team often becomes re-energized. The final responsibilities that remain are simple and straightforward, yet are loaded with the promise of true performance improvement. The team must prepare its project report and make its final presentation to the quality oversight group.

Report Findings and Recommendations

It is advantageous, and fairly customary, for improvement project teams to present the findings and recommendations of their work in both written and oral forms. The written report should include a copy of the original project design document, as well as new information. Specifically, the final project team report should offer a substantive summary of the team's efforts, a clear explanation of the reasons for current performance, a prioritized list of suggested improvements, and a preliminary plan for testing the identified improvements.

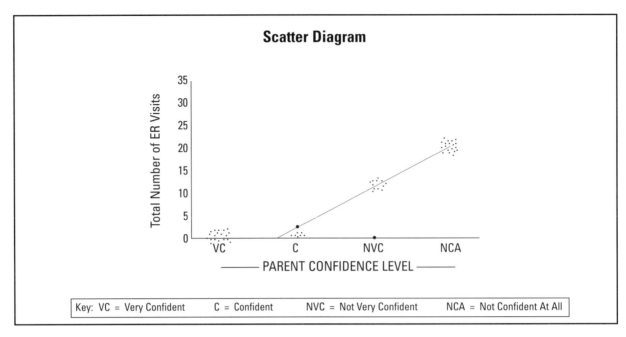

Figure 5-7. *This scatter diagram illustrates the relationship between parent's level of confidence and return of the post-T & A child to the emergency room. Of the 19 parents who were very confident in their ability to care for their child, 0 made an emergency room visit; of the 8 parents who were confident in their ability to care for their child, 1 made an emergency room visit; of the 13 parents who were not very confident in their ability to care for their child, 12 made an emergency room visit; and of the 19 parents who were not confident at all, all 19 made an emergency room visit.*

EXERCISE BREAK

Take a few moments to review Worksheet #10: Improvement Team Final Report, which is on page 159 in the Appendix. Compare this form to the final written report from an improvement project in which you were involved. Did your final report present all the information identified on this form? If not, what was missing? Why was it not included? Did your final report include additional information that is not specified on this report? If so, why was it included? How would you modify this report so that it meets the unique needs of your organization? You may also find it helpful to review this worksheet at the outset of a new performance measurement and improvement project and to use it or a modified version for your final report.

Improvement teams frequently design storyboards that present a visual summary of their work. Included on the storyboard are definition of the improvement opportunity, graphical or tabular display of current performance, summary of performance causes, recommended improvements, and members of the team. The storyboard is often structured according to the steps in the organization's performance improvement methodology. Storyboards are frequently placed in high traffic areas of the organization so that as many staff (and patients) as possible can see the improvement project.

The oral presentation of the project to the quality oversight body typically follows the format of the written report. During this live presentation, the project team has a chance to respond to queries or concerns. The team can also receive direct and immediate feedback about their project work. Another important function of such a formal presentation is that it begins to bring closure to the team-based component of the improvement project. It creates a natural opportunity for the project team to hand-off responsibility for testing and implementing improvements to the line management and staff who "own" the service and work processes.

Improving Organization Performance

Once the outcomes-based performance improvement project team has made their final report to the quality oversight body, it becomes that group's responsibility to determine which of the improvement suggestions are aligned with the high-priority, strategic improvement objectives of the organization and should, therefore, be tested expediently. (If the executive sponsor of the team has fulfilled the oversight and coaching role responsibilities appropriately, all recommended improvements should be of high priority.)

The Plan-Do-Check-Act (PDCA) Cycle

The quality oversight body must also ensure that all improvement ideas are systematically tested using whatever specific testing model or approach the organization has selected. A common test model that has been used successfully by many institutions, including ambulatory care organizations, is the Plan-Do-Check-Act (PDCA) Cycle.

Application of the PDCA Cycle is relatively uncomplicated. During the *plan phase,* a specific action plan for testing the improvement idea on a small scale is drafted. Such a plan should detail

■ what specific changes will be tested;

■ how the changes will be tested;

■ who needs to be involved in the test;

■ what the involved individuals need to know or do to participate in the test;

■ when the test will be initiated;

■ how long the test period will last; and

■ how the impact of the tested change will be evaluated.

The *do phase* of the PDCA cycle is the time when the test is actually conducted and the effects of the improvement idea are measured. The *check phase* occurs when the results of the test are analyzed. Four potential outcomes of a test of an improvement idea are possible. The tested change may lead to performance that is improved, unchanged, declined, or unclear.

The *act phase* of the PDCA cycle implements appropriate follow-up from the test. Three types of actions are taken as a result of the outcomes of the test:

1. If performance has been improved, the change is institutionalized and becomes part of the way the organization routinely does its work. A decision may be made to test one or more new improvement ideas.

2. If performance is unchanged or declined, the effect of the test is documented and, obviously, no process changes are initiated. However, a decision may be made to initiate a test of one or more other improvement ideas.

3. If performance is unclear, re-examining how the impact of the tested change was evaluated is unnecessary. It is essential to reconsider the relationship between the tested change and the outcome. Perhaps a positive correlation appeared to exist when, in fact, it did not. At this point, it must be decided if retesting the same change would yield any different or more useful information. If so, a retest may be conducted. If not, the decision to test one or more additional changes may be made.

As tests are completed and changes implemented, the quality oversight group, in association with line managers, must decide how to implement routine performance measurement in the areas that have been improved. Performance in these areas must be monitored in an ongoing fashion, to be sure that the gains made are sustained.

THOUGHT BREAK

■ *Consider the implementation of improvements in your organization.*

■ *Do you have a consistent approach for testing and assessing the impact of all improvement ideas?*

■ *Are improvement ideas routinely tested on a small scale before widespread implementation or organization change?*

■ *If not, has the failure to test an improvement led to unwanted results?*

■ *What does your organization need to do to become better at consistently evaluating improvement suggestions?*

Communicating Findings

When genuine improvements have been achieved, it is cause for communication and celebration. Organizations have many existing internal and external communication channels. Opportunities for corporate learning are also generally plentiful.

Staff should be routinely informed about the status of different performance improvement initiatives. When specific processes, practices, protocols, procedures or policies change, staff in-servicing will be necessary. Giving public recognition to improvement teams whose work has led to meaningful improvement is appropriate. Newsletters, memos, storyboards, teaching bulletin boards, paycheck stuffers, and e-mail announcements are just a few of the possible ways of informing staff. Organization board members should also be updated on the significant improvements that have been made. Often, this information is included in a performance report that is prepared for scheduled board meetings or for an annual report.

Equally as important as internal communication is communication with external stakeholders, including patients, their families/friends, the surrounding community, purchasers, payers, regulators, accreditors, professional associations, and other practicing professionals. When communicating with these external groups, it is important to know what their vested interests are, what information about organization performance they need, how they use such information, and their general levels of understanding about performance improvement and ambulatory health care service delivery and outcomes. Organization newsletters and community events announcements go a long way in disseminating general information and promoting a positive organization image. They may not, however, meet the information needs or wants of some of your organization's most important stakeholders. In such situations, it is highly beneficial to work together with those information users to prepare information dissemination or communication structures that meet their unique needs.

Key Points

1. All performance measurement and improvement initiatives should be planned. Planning should reveal the origins of the project, define and validate the project purpose, specify the desired effect of the project, develop project success measures, specify necessary resources, describe any constraints, anticipate problems, and specify milestones and deadlines.

2. An interdisciplinary team is usually created to implement the improvement project. This team is generally composed of staff from different disciplines, organization entities, and levels throughout the facility.

3. An improvement team is typically composed of an executive coach, a team leader, a facilitator, and multiple team members. Sometimes a measurement specialist is included in the team. Additional subject matter experts serve as ad hoc team members, as needed.

4. Data management is a process composed of the following discrete activities: determination of data needs, specification of indicators, definition of data elements, specification of data sources, creation of data collection instruments, determination of data analysis strategies, completion of a data collection plan, pilot testing data collection and analysis, and modification of data management tactics based on the results of the pilot test.

5. Two fundamental kinds of studies exist: quantitative and qualitative. Quantitative studies present numeric performance data, such as averages, correlations, and variation. Qualitative studies provide narrative data, such as content and theme analyses and individual quotes.

6. Effective data collection requires valid and reliable data collection instruments and trained data collectors.

7. Analysis of performance data may be quantitative or qualitative and compare organization performance to itself, over time, and to external benchmarks.

8. Root cause analysis employs tools such as the process flow diagram, cause-effect diagram, scatter diagram, Pareto analysis, and

Repetitive Why? to determine the causes of achieved performance.

9. Improvement ideas should be tested on a small scale, using a systematic approach such as the Plan-Do-Check-Act (PDCA) Cycle.

10. Findings and results of performance measurement and improvement initiatives should be communicated to internal and external audiences via a variety of approaches.

References

1. Joint Commission on Accreditation of Healthcare Organizations: *The Measurement Mandate.* Oakbrook Terrace, IL, 1993, pp 150–151.

2. Spendolini MJ: *The Benchmarking Book.* Chicago: American Management Association, 1992, pp 7–15.

Chapter 6:

Designing an Outcomes Measurement Project: A Self-Directed Learning Exercise

This chapter offers an opportunity to design an outcomes measurement project for a fictitious ambulatory care organization.

Instructions

1. You may complete this exercise individually or in a group.

2. Read the following description of the First Choice Community Clinic (FCCC)*.

3. Assume you are a consultant engaged by the clinic to develop a high-impact outcomes measurement project.

4. Review what you know about this organization's performance.

5. Determine what additional performance information you would like to have. Offer your consultee an explanation of why this missing information would be useful.

6. Consider your list of desired performance information and the reason(s) you think each area of missing information is important. Select the three most critical areas of missing information. Share with your consultee your rationale(s) for choosing these three areas.

7. For each of these three areas, develop the outcomes measures that are needed to generate the information you desire. When developing your measures, be sure to define all data elements and specify all data sources. Explain to your consultee why/how these specific measures will provide the desired information.

8. Create the collection tools that will be used to record the data for each of your outcomes measures. Be sure to include any special data collection instructions on each tool.

9. Describe the data analysis methods for each of your measures. Depending on the nature of the measure, consider averages, rates, standard deviations, run charts, control charts, histograms, thematic content analysis, descriptive summaries, and so forth. Explain to your consultee why the data analysis methods you selected are the most appropriate and useful.

10. Draft a preliminary data collection and analysis action plan. Specify who are the most appropriate data collectors, when data should be collected, who is most appropriate to analyze data, and when data analysis should begin and end.

11. You may use the worksheets included at the end of this chapter to record your work.

Note: There is no "correct" answer to this exercise. The strongest responses have clear, logical, and informed rationales. These instruction numbers correspond to the worksheets at the end of this chapter.

The Organization

The First Choice Community Clinic is an inner city ambulatory health care center currently providing general medical, obstetric/gynecologic, pediatric, and mental health care to a primarily indigent population. Clinic staff offer disease management, illness prevention, and health promotion services. The health center's mission is to provide high-quality, low-cost health care services that improve the health of individuals and the community as a whole.

---

* The First Choice Community Clinic (FCCC) is a fictitious organization. Any resemblance to an actual ambulatory care organization is strictly coincidental.

The clinic was established by two nurse practitioners (NP) and a certified nurse midwife (CNM) in the early 1980's as part of a national effort to provide health care to under-served populations. Start-up dollars for providing basic management of chronic and acute illnesses and prenatal care were received through grants from public funding sources.

The health center has grown since its early days, when "drop-in" patients came to see the advanced nurse practitioners (ANPs) who were available for three hours each day, five days a week. As residents from the surrounding community gained trust in the nurses, the number of patients seeking health services grew.

Having moved twice, from the original storefront facility to office space provided by a local church, the clinic is now permanently located in a street-level suite of offices donated by a local business. Today, FCCC is a cornerstone in the landscape of this impoverished community.

The health center serves a variety of patients with differing needs. High-volume services include maternity care, general pediatrics, geriatrics, ongoing treatment of chronic illnesses (such as diabetes and hypertension), and episodic care for the full spectrum of acute illnesses and health problems. High-risk services include treatment of patients with infectious diseases (such as AIDS and tuberculosis), substance abuse treatment, medical and mental health care for victims of domestic violence, and outpatient management of depression. The clinic averages 1,100 patient visits each month.

Most clinic patients are recipients of Medicaid or Medicare. Reimbursement for delivered services does not generate the income necessary to maintain financial solvency. Utilization management is an ongoing challenge.

The center has been consistently successful in renewing existing grants and winning new ones. Although it continues to rely on sources of public money, primary financial support now comes through grants from private organizations and philanthropic contributions. Donors are cultivated by the clinic board and designated staff. The clinic's initially tenuous financial status has

stabilized. At present, operating expenses are manageable and a small financial reserve has been built. The ability to implement planned expansions in services is contingent upon a continuing influx of unrestricted contributions.

Over time, health center hours, services, and staff have expanded. The clinic is currently open Monday through Saturday for approximately 60 hours each week. Appointments are preferred, although walk-in patients with urgent conditions will be seen.

The center's core health services (medical, ob/gyn, pediatrics, and mental health) are offered every day. Specialty clinics, such as well baby check-ups and pediatric immunizations, are scheduled several times each month. Patient education classes, such as preparing for childbirth, how to parent, basic nutrition, self-management of diabetes, and coping with being a teen are also offered at pre-set times each month. Groups offering psychosocial support to individuals with specific needs are prescheduled. Two parental stress groups are offered each week. An HIV+ support group and a victims of violence group are offered every other week. An Alcoholics Anonymous meeting is held in the center's offices one evening each week.

The First Choice Community Clinic currently employs 19 full and part-time staff, including

- two part-time receptionists;
- one part-time medical records technician;
- two full-time and one part-time NP;
- one full-time and two part-time CNMs;
- one full-time mental health clinical nurse specialist;
- one part-time physician's assistant (PA);
- one full-time family practice physician;
- one part-time obstetrician/gynecologist;
- one part-time pediatrician;
- one full-time accounting coordinator;
- one part-time reimbursement specialist;
- one part-time fund development specialist;
- one full-time medical director; and
- one full-time clinic administrator (who is a nurse).

All clinic physicians are on staff at local hospitals. Patients are referred, as needed, to medical subspecialists who have agreed to work with the health center's patients. Patients are also referred to tertiary care centers for the treatment of severe and complicated health problems.

Housekeeping, maintenance, and security services are subcontracted. A small group of community residents serve as volunteers, primarily performing clerical tasks. Volunteers from the local religious institutions provide pastoral care services on an as-needed basis.

Clinic staff are building bridges to academic health centers in the city, with hopes of becoming a clinical practicum site for nursing and medical students.

The FCCC Board of Directors is composed of one elected community resident representative, five representatives from the business and health care communities in the city, and the health center's medical and administrative directors. The primary function of the board is to provide direction and offer guidance on strategic issues. It ensures that all the activities and initiatives in which the center engages will lead to the successful achievement of the organization's mission and goals.

The health center is in full compliance with all pertinent regulatory requirements. To the greatest extent possible, it strives to comply with accreditation standards. It has not yet sought accreditation, primarily for financial reasons. However, accreditation within the next five years is a high priority strategic goal.

How the Organization Currently Measures Its Performance

Both the clinical and administrative staff of the center believe that patients receive excellent care. Most patients get well or get better. Anecdotal feedback from patients is generally positive. Although there are sometimes problems "getting the job done," staff have discovered ways to successfully work around them. A common view is that these problems could be solved and the clinic's performance could be made even better if more money was available.

Because clinical outcomes measurement at the First Choice Community Clinic is very limited at this time, there are little objective data to demonstrate achieved patient outcomes. Therefore, discussions about patient outcomes are generally highly subjective and based on personal experiences, perceptions, and opinions. When clinical outcomes data are available, they have typically been collected as part of a grant application process. An area of exception is infection control. Infection control data include numbers and types of reportable infectious diseases in patients/staff and type/occurrence of disease outbreaks.

Measurement and assessment of key clinical processes is also minimal at the present time. There are little data describing patient access to service, assessment and identification of the patient's health problems and needs, treatment and care, patient education, integration of care across providers and service sites, and patient follow-up. *Infection control* data, however, present numbers and types of administered pediatric and geriatric immunizations.

Measurement of nonclinical outcomes and processes is more common. *Financial* data that are collected include revenue, expenses, variations from budget, total assets and liabilities, and distribution and use of restricted/unrestricted grant and donor funds. *Utilization* data include total numbers of patients seen, patients seen by service, and patients seen per practitioner; numbers of on-site lab studies and off-site diagnostic procedures; total numbers of internal referrals, number of internal referrals to billable services, number of internal referrals to non-billable services; numbers of and reasons for external referrals; and tracking of reimbursements and denials of payment. *Medical records* data include total number of incomplete patient records each month, incomplete patient records by practitioner, and incomplete patient records by type of information missing. *Human resources* data include number of patient referrals to each medical subspecialist consultant, sick time usage, turnover rate, ratio of full-time to part-time employees, and demonstrated competencies for each staff person.

Available *risk management* data include incident data: total number of incidents, number of patient incidents, number of staff incidents, incidents categorized by type, descriptive summaries of each incident and how it was managed, and number and nature of patient complaints.

Some *quality control* data are available, such as specification limits of lab analyzers for hematology, blood chemistries and urine analysis; calibration of blood glucose meters; and expiration dates of medications and drug samples.

Instruction #5. Desired Additional Performance Information Worksheet

List the additional performance information you would like. State why it would be useful to have this information.

Additional Information

Reason it is Useful

Instruction #6. Most Critical Areas of Information Worksheet

From your list of desired additional performance information, select the three most critical areas of missing information. Explain your rationale for choosing each of these areas.

Most Critical Areas   **Rationale**

1. _____   _____

   _____   _____

   _____   _____

   _____   _____

2. _____   _____

   _____   _____

   _____   _____

   _____   _____

3. _____   _____

   _____   _____

   _____   _____

   _____   _____

Instruction #7. Developing Outcomes Measures Worksheet

Develop all the outcomes measures necessary to produce the information in your three most critical areas of missing information. Define all data elements. Indicate all data sources. Explain why or how these measures will provide the desired information.

Outcomes Measures/ Data Elements	Data Sources	Explanation

Instruction #9. Data Analysis Methods Worksheet

Describe the data analysis methods for each of your developed outcomes measures.

Outcomes Measure   **Data Analysis Method**

_____   _____
_____   _____
_____   _____
_____   _____
_____   _____
_____   _____
_____   _____
_____   _____
_____   _____
_____   _____
_____   _____
_____   _____
_____   _____
_____   _____
_____   _____
_____   _____
_____   _____
_____   _____
_____   _____
_____   _____
_____   _____
_____   _____
_____   _____
_____   _____
_____   _____
_____   _____
_____   _____
_____   _____
_____   _____
_____   _____
_____   _____
_____   _____
_____   _____
_____   _____
_____   _____
_____   _____
_____   _____
_____   _____
_____   _____
_____   _____

Instruction #10. Data Collection and Analysis Action Plan Worksheet

Complete the following preliminary data collection and analysis action plan.

Data To Be Collected	By Whom	Start/End

Data To Be Analyzed	By Whom	Start/End

Chapter 7:

Case Stories

> **This chapter presents two case stories of outcomes-focused performance improvement projects:**
>
> ■ The first story examines how a United States Air Force hospital improved patient outcomes, achieved efficiencies in operations, and reduced operating expenses in its cardiology clinic.
>
> ■ The second story describes how the Pain Management Service of an academic health system compared the clinical and cost outcomes of conservative and aggressive treatment for patients with radicular low back pain who were receiving workers' compensation benefits.

Introduction

The following case stories are intended to enliven the theoretical concepts presented in this book.

The first case story explores how the services of an extensive yet unintegrated cardiology service are reviewed, aligned, integrated, and shifted from an inpatient to an outpatient treatment model. Although Wilford-Hall Medical Center is a large military institution, it experiences serious resource limitations. This example illustrates how meaningful improvements can be achieved through simple approaches that require little measurement or statistical expertise or highly advanced technological support. The Wilford-Hall story shows how creatively spreading existing resources around identified patient needs and expectations can simultaneously produce improved clinical, satisfaction, and business results.

The second story, from the pain management service at the University of Massachusetts Memorial Health Care System, demonstrates how one person can conduct practice-changing performance improvement initiatives. It describes how a nurse factually demonstrated the improved clinical and economic outcomes resulting from the use of epidural steroid injections for pain control in patients with chronic low back pain. She developed this project in response to her own curiosity about the impact of different treatment approaches. Her curiosity saved her more than $1.5 million.

Each story begins with a brief description of the organization and its performance improvement philosophy. A detailed summary of the outcomes measurement project and the study goals are then presented. Next, the data collection method and the data analysis strategies are explained. A description of how this effort led to real improvement is then presented. Finally, the "lessons learned" as a consequence of each project are enumerated.

Although each story is unique, both show the power of performance measurement. The driving goal of each is to improve their organization's performance by consistently achieving better patient outcomes. *That* is the real benefit of understanding and applying the principles and concepts of performance measurement.

Case Story #1:
Case Story #1:
Wilford-Hall Medical Center—
Doing "Whatever It Takes" to
Improve Ambulatory Cardiac Services

What Is Wilford-Hall Medical Center?

Wilford-Hall Medical Center (WHMC) is located on Lackland Air Force Base in San Antonio, Texas. Active military personnel, retirees, and their family members receive comprehensive, state-of-the-art care in more than 135 medical specialties and subspecialties. With approximately 2,000 inpatient admissions and 84,000 visits in its clinics and dispensaries each month, WHMC is the largest medical facility in the United States Air Force. In addition, as a Level I Trauma Center, WHMC provides emergency and trauma care to civilians from surrounding communities.

The **vision** of Wilford-Hall Medical Center is to be able, at any time, to provide and deploy the continuum of healthcare services across the world. To achieve this desired state, the medical center is committed to the four major purposes described in their **mission**:

■ *Readiness:* The medical center is ever-ready to support global engagement by providing and deploying healthcare services under the challenging conditions of the worldwide contingencies;

■ *Peacetime Healthcare:* The medical center demonstrates its commitment to building healthier communities by consistently delivering compassionate, personalized health-care services;

■ *Education and Training:* As the primary provider of Air Force-sponsored health services education and training, the medical center enables the delivery of optimal healthcare to support peacetime and readiness missions; and

■ *Research:* As the foremost healthcare research site in the Air Force, the medical center strives to improve peacetime and readiness capabilities by routinely conducting numerous clinical investigations involving the simultaneous implementation of hundreds of active research protocols.

The critical work of mission fulfillment at WHMC occurs in a **values**-driven environment that prizes integrity, service before self, and excellence. These values are made real in "can do" behaviors that visibly demonstrate the "Whatever It Takes!" facility **motto**. It is in this culture of personal responsibility and accountability that the strategic goals and objectives of WHMC can be realized.

What Does Performance Improvement Mean at Wilford-Hall Medical Center?

Performance improvement at WHMC is based on Quality Air Force (QAF), the Air Force approach to total quality management. This approach

■ is based on the Malcolm Baldrige National Quality Award criteria;

■ offers a conceptual framework for measuring, assessing, improving, and sustaining performance;

■ expects performance improvement initiatives to be aligned with the mission, vision, and strategic plans of the Air Force and the medical facility;

■ demands leadership commitment;

■ requires an operating style that inspires trust, teamwork, and continuous improvement;

■ values multidisciplinary teams;

■ supports process design/redesign efforts;

■ expects process improvements to lead to better results;

■ emphasizes the achievement of outcomes that meet or exceed the needs and expectations of patients, staff, and other key customers; and

■ endorses FOCUS-PDCA as the chosen improvement methodology.

WHMC uses Departmental Process Analysis (DPA) in conjunction with FOCUS-PDCA to conduct departmental improvement projects. DPA is a tool that provides a structured way of transitioning from traditional problem solving to process improvement. Grounded in an appreciation of the links between processes and outcomes, DPA facilitates an evolution from management by results to management by study

FOCUS-PDCA

FOCUS-PDCA was developed by the Hospital Corporation of America, which is now a part of the Columbia Health Care Corporation. FOCUS, an acronym, stands for

1. **F**ind a process to improve;
2. **O**rganize a team that knows the process;
3. **C**larify current knowledge of the process;
4. **U**nderstand causes of process variation; and
5. **S**elect the process improvement.

The PDCA cycle is also known as the Shewhart cycle or the Deming cycle. It was developed by Walther Shewhart, a leader in the development of modern statistical quality control. The PDCA cycle offers a systematic and organized approach for testing improvement actions. PDCA stands for

1. **P**lan pilot test of the prospective improvement action;
2. **D**o the pilot test;
3. **C**heck the results of the pilot test; and
4. **A**ct on the results of the pilot test.

and improvement of processes. It includes the following ten steps:

1. Identify the department's mission and link it to the organization's mission.
2. Identify each of your key suppliers and specify what you need from them.
3. Identify each of your key customers and specify what they need from you.
4. Identify your key processes.
5. Prioritize your key processes.
6. Verify your key processes with your customers.
7. Macro-flowchart your key processes.
8. Select a process to study.
9. Initiate FOCUS-PDCA.
10. Plan for continuous DPA.

What Is the Cardiology Services Improvement Project?

The Cardiology Division at WHMC has a mission and vision that are aligned with the overall mission and vision of the medical center.

Mission:

- To provide the highest quality, most cost-effective cardiovascular care;
- Empower all individuals to operate at the highest level of military and medical professionalism;

- Maintain a fighting force capable of sustaining worldwide operations;
- Strive for excellence in all operations; and
- Maximize the full potential of the staff and the division through education, training, and research.

Vision: Best quality, best service, best cost.

Cast against this backdrop, the Cardiology Division was challenged by administrators to respond to compelling external forces demanding that military health care facilities achieve the best possible clinical outcomes while simultaneously reducing costs. Committed to successfully accomplishing this charge, cardiology staff used their empirical experience to identify several overarching divisionwide improvement goals.

Beginning with the commitment to exceed the standards of the Cardiology Boards, these improvement goals were designed to

1. improve or maintain patient outcomes, including health status (symptom amelioration or control, positive response to therapeutic interventions, minimization of complications, and reduced morbidity and mortality) and well-being (patient's own sense of health, strength, functionality, and competence to manage necessary self care activities);

2. improve patient satisfaction with care and services, specifically addressing access, timeliness, coordination, and continuity;

3. manage costs/decrease expenses by

   a. actively managing resource utilization to eliminate medically unnecessary days,

   b. developing and implementing new care models that transition cardiac services from inpatient to outpatient settings, to the greatest extent possible, and

   c. achieving and sustaining efficiencies in the operation of key clinical and non-clinical processes, such as diagnostic testing and scheduling of services and procedures;

4. move toward an integrated product line model of cardiovascular care; and

5. maintain resource neutrality.

After identifying these broad, driving goals, cardiology division staff

1. identified and flowcharted each step in the patient care/services processes;

2. developed and administered a survey asking patients to

   a. rate in importance (to them) each of the identified steps in the processes of receiving care and services, and

   b. indicate their degree of satisfaction with their experience at each step;

3. reinforced, based on patient feedback, the need for service consolidation or "one-stop shopping" to eliminate patients' experience of fragmented cardiology services;

4. based on patient feedback, reinforced the need to

   a. streamline key components of critical patient-focused processes, such as scheduling and completing prescribed procedures (for instance, a 90-day backlog of 300 echocardiograms was discovered; this unacceptably long waiting period sometimes resulted in inpatient admissions in order for patients to receive a more timely echocardiogram), and

   b. eliminate complexity in the admission and discharge processes; and

5. collected baseline data about diagnoses, lengths of stay, and care costs for key services, such as inpatient cardiac catheterizations and care of patients with chest pain.

Division staff were mindful of the need to use wisely the resources available for performance improvement activities. Because of that awareness, they elected to conduct a manageable number of improvement projects. Based on the review of patient feedback, initial examination of performance data, and empirical experience, cardiology division staff selected three specific improvement projects:

1. Operations of the Cardiology Clinics and Noninvasive Laboratories;

2. Ratio of inpatient to outpatient cardiac catheterizations; and

3. Management of patients with chest pain.

What Were the Goals of the Three Cardiology Services Improvement Projects?

Project #1: *Operations of the Cardiology Clinics and Non-invasive Laboratories*

Goals:
1. Achieve and sustain a complication ratio for non-invasive procedures at less than the national occurrence rate.

2. Improve access (decrease wait times for routine, urgent, and emergency consultations and eliminate backlogs in the echocardiology lab) and continuity of care (develop a way to efficiently and effectively transfer accurate clinical information across the continuum of cardiac care).

3. Increase throughput (productivity; total number of patients seen and number of patients seen per provider).

4. Maintain or improve the quality of cardiac studies.

5. Improve patient perception of care and satisfaction with services.

6. Develop a cardiology computer network to improve access to

clinical information, efficiency, and productivity.

7. Develop and implement an outreach program to accommodate military medical services referrals.

8. Increase staff satisfaction with task mix, workload, and professional learning and growth.

Project #2: *Ratio between inpatient and outpatient cardiac catheterizations*

Goals:

1. Achieve and sustain a cardiac catheterization complication ratio less than the national occurrence rate.

2. Use National Institutes of Health guidelines on the management of unstable angina to determine when to transfer patients to the chest pain unit.

3. Use Interqual criteria to decrease admissions to the Coronary Care Unit (CCU).

4. Eliminate inappropriate postprocedure admission of outpatients.

5. Meet the civilian sector's standard of practice for outpatient/same day cardiac catheterizations.

6. Decrease costs (by decreasing lengths of stay and increasing same day/< 24-hour admissions and discharges).

7. Maintain or improve the quality of cardiac catheterization studies.

8. Eliminate complexity from the preadmission process.

9. Improve patient satisfaction with the preadmission process.

Project #3: *Management of patients with chest pain*

Goals:

1. Maintain or improve the myocardial infarction and mortality rates in patients with chest pain.

2. Transition the observation of patients with chest pain from an inpatient to an outpatient setting.

3. Eliminate inappropriate admission of patients with chest pain to the CCU.

4. Align practice with the recommendations and standards of professional associations.

5. Initiate 72-hour follow-up of patients discharged from the chest pain unit. Improve patient access to appropriate levels of care.

6. Improve overall patient satisfaction with the discharge and follow-up processes.

7. Decrease costs by decreasing service intensity and lengths of stay.

What Data Were Collected?

A variety of data collection strategies, such as face-to-face discussions with patients and staff, direct observation, and record or report abstraction, were employed. Members of multi-disciplinary improvement teams collected data via surveys, questionnaires, check sheets, logs, and focused discussion groups. Approaches to data collection were based on the specific types of data that were needed.

Data sources included various databases such as the cardiac catheterization lab database, corporate executive information system (CEIS) database, and database spreadsheets. Additional data sources included manual logs from different sections of the Cardiology Division, utilization management reports, patient records, documented performance capabilities and specifications for biomedical devices, the Department of Defense Patient Survey, admitting and discharge reports, and credentials review and privileging records. Patients and staff provided important qualitative data that reflected their perceptions and experiences.

General patient satisfaction data are routinely collected. Figure 7-1, pages 112–113, is an example of a patient satisfaction survey used in the Division of Cardiology at WHMC. *Patients' perceptions in relation to specific procedures* are also assessed. Figure 7-2, page 114, is an example of

Division of Cardiology, Wilford-Hall Medical Center
OUTPATIENT QUESTIONNAIRE

CLINIC YOU WERE VISITING: ❏ Cardiology   ❏ Coumadin   ❏ AICD/Pacemaker

We are proud of the Division of Cardiology and continually try to improve the care and service we provide to you. Each time you share your opinion of the care you received during your visit, you help us identify our strengths and weaknesses. Your input is valuable to us, and we strive to make any improvement you may recommend. Please leave your completed form with hospital personnel, or deposit in the questionnaire box.

ROBERT M. SAAD, LTC USAF, MC
Commander, Division of Cardiology

Fill in appropriate column: ❏ Male   ❏ Active Duty   ❏ A/D Family
                                  ❏ Female   ❏ Retired   ❏ Ret Family

Name (Optional)_____   ❏ Other (Specify)_____

Phone#_____   Date of Appointment_____

Beside each question you will find two sets of horizonal columns to rate your care. The first set rates or reflects your satisfaction with the care received, and the second rates or reflects the importance of the question to you.

Using a scale of 1-5, with *5* being *high satisfaction* with your care or a *very important* item in your care and *1* being *low satisfaction* or an item of *low importance* **in your care, please rate your care by marking the appropriate box.**

	SATISFACTION					IMPORTANCE				
1. APPOINTMENT SYSTEM:	**1**	**2**	**3**	**4**	**5**	**1**	**2**	**3**	**4**	**5**
a. Time it took to reach appointment clerk	❏	❏	❏	❏	❏	❏	❏	❏	❏	❏
b. Availability of appointment phone number(s)	❏	❏	❏	❏	❏	❏	❏	❏	❏	❏
c. Reasonableness of appointment time	❏	❏	❏	❏	❏	❏	❏	❏	❏	❏
d. Courtesy of appointment clerks	❏	❏	❏	❏	❏	❏	❏	❏	❏	❏
2. ENVIRONMENTAL/FACILITY:	**1**	**2**	**3**	**4**	**5**	**1**	**2**	**3**	**4**	**5**
a. Directional signs	❏	❏	❏	❏	❏	❏	❏	❏	❏	❏
b. Physical access:										
1. To clinics	❏	❏	❏	❏	❏	❏	❏	❏	❏	❏
2. To reception/check-in desk	❏	❏	❏	❏	❏	❏	❏	❏	❏	❏
3. To exam rooms	❏	❏	❏	❏	❏	❏	❏	❏	❏	❏
4. To check-out (appointments, lab slips, and so forth)	❏	❏	❏	❏	❏	❏	❏	❏	❏	❏
5. To laboratories for procedures	❏	❏	❏	❏	❏	❏	❏	❏	❏	❏
c. Cleanliness of waiting area	❏	❏	❏	❏	❏	❏	❏	❏	❏	❏

continued on next page

Figure 7-1. *This figure presents the satisfaction survey administered to patients in the cardiology clinics at Wilford-Hall Medical Center.* ***Source:*** *Wilford-Hall Medical Center. Used with permission.*

	SATISFACTION					IMPORTANCE				
3. RECEPTION:	**1**	**2**	**3**	**4**	**5**	**1**	**2**	**3**	**4**	**5**
a. Waiting time	❏	❏	❏	❏	❏	❏	❏	❏	❏	❏
b. Cleanliness of waiting area	❏	❏	❏	❏	❏	❏	❏	❏	❏	❏
c. Courtesy of reception personnel	❏	❏	❏	❏	❏	❏	❏	❏	❏	❏
d. Explanation of delays	❏	❏	❏	❏	❏	❏	❏	❏	❏	❏

4. CLINICS: (Mark Clinic Visited) ❏ Cardiology ❏ Coumadin ❏ AICD/Pacemaker

	1	**2**	**3**	**4**	**5**	**1**	**2**	**3**	**4**	**5**
a. Explanation of delays (if applicable)	❏	❏	❏	❏	❏	❏	❏	❏	❏	❏
b. Introduction to providers/support personnel	❏	❏	❏	❏	❏	❏	❏	❏	❏	❏
c. Physician response										
1. Explains care/treatment/tests	❏	❏	❏	❏	❏	❏	❏	❏	❏	❏
2. Meets physical and emotional needs	❏	❏	❏	❏	❏	❏	❏	❏	❏	❏
3. Responds to patient privacy	❏	❏	❏	❏	❏	❏	❏	❏	❏	❏
4. Listens to what patient says	❏	❏	❏	❏	❏	❏	❏	❏	❏	❏
5. Discusses disease with patient/family	❏	❏	❏	❏	❏	❏	❏	❏	❏	❏
6. Explains medications to patient/family	❏	❏	❏	❏	❏	❏	❏	❏	❏	❏
7. Physician caring, respectful, courteous	❏	❏	❏	❏	❏	❏	❏	❏	❏	❏
d. Comfort with physician's knowledge/training	❏	❏	❏	❏	❏	❏	❏	❏	❏	❏
e. Support personnel (nurses and technicians)										
1. Listens to what the patient says	❏	❏	❏	❏	❏	❏	❏	❏	❏	❏
2. Meets physical and emotional needs	❏	❏	❏	❏	❏	❏	❏	❏	❏	❏
3. Responds to patient privacy	❏	❏	❏	❏	❏	❏	❏	❏	❏	❏
4. Caring, respectful, courteous	❏	❏	❏	❏	❏	❏	❏	❏	❏	❏
f. Exam room cleanliness, orderliness	❏	❏	❏	❏	❏	❏	❏	❏	❏	❏

	1	**2**	**3**	**4**	**5**	**1**	**2**	**3**	**4**	**5**
5. FOLLOW-UP INFORMATION BY HEALTH CARE PROVIDER:										
a. Received follow-up information (i.e., test results, and so on) from health care provider in a reasonable time	❏	❏	❏	❏	❏	❏	❏	❏	❏	❏

6. Comments

_____
_____
_____
_____
_____
_____

a postprocedure assessment log used in the Cardiac Catheterization Lab. Clinic staff use this log to record patient responses to the listed trigger items. *Clinical outcomes data,* such as complication and mortality rates, are collected. *Operations outcomes measures* track such things as wait times from first patient contact to first clinic visit, backlogs, and provider productivity.

Other outcomes measures calculate length of stay, inpatient to outpatient ratios, and costs of care. Data related to specific improvement projects are also collected. Examples of measures for each of the three Division of Cardiology improvement projects are presented in Table 7-1, page 115.

Postprocedure Assessment Log—Cardiac Catheterization Laboratory								
Procedure:								
Date of Procedure:								
Date of Postprocedure Assessment:								
	Y/N/NA	Y/N/NA	Y/N/NA	Y/N/NA	Y/N/NA	Y/N/NA	Y/N/NA	Y/N/NA
1) Satisfaction with Service:								
a) Caring, Professional Environment								
b) Privacy Respected for Procedure								
c) Physician Explanation Adequate Prior to Consent								
d) Nurse/Technician Explanation Adequate/Timely								
e) Were You Reasonably Comfortable During the Procedure								
f) Suggestions for Improvement*								
2) Catheter Insertion Site:								
a) Unusual bleeding or drainage to Cath Site								
b) Unusual Redness to Site								
c) Unusual Bruising to Site								
d) Swelling (larger than size of olive)								
3) Limb(s) distal to Insertion Site:								
a) Numbness/Tingling								
b) Cool								
4) Fever/Chills								
5) Able to Resume Previous Diet								
6) Able to Resume Previous Activities								
7) Discharge Instructions:								
a) Adequate Instructions to Follow During Bedrest Recovery Period								
b) Received Printed Discharge Instructions Prior to Discharge								
8) Follow-Up Appointment with Cardiologist/PCM Arranged Prior to Discharge								
9) Any Unscheduled Hospital Admissions/ER or Clinic Visits Since Discharge								
Not able to contact pt. (list # of attempts)								
* Attach Narrative								

Figure 7-2. *This Postprocedure Assessment Log is used to document a follow-up patient assessment, post-cardiac catheterization.* **Source:** *Wilford-Hall Medical Center. Used with permission.*

Table 7-1. Examples* of Measures for the Three Performance Improvement Projects Implemented by the Division of Cardiology at Wilford-Hall Medical Center

IMPROVEMENT PROJECT	DATA
Operations of the Cardiology Clinics and Non-Invasive Laboratories	# of clinic visits # of noninvasive procedures Procedure complications Completeness of patient preparation for procedure Indications for procedure Appropriateness of new patient referrals Appropriateness of referral for procedure Consultation backlogs Noninvasive procedure backlogs

Ratio of inpatient to outpatient cardiac catheterizations	Total # of cardiac caths
	# of inpatient procedures
	# of outpatient procedures
	# for specific purposes:
	    Angioplasty
	    Revascularization
	    AICD/pacemaker implants
	    EPS studies and ablations
	    Elective cardioversions
	    Transesophageal echoes
	Myocardial infarction rates
	Complication type and rates
	Mortality rates
	% of outpatients admitted to:
	    Coronary care unit (CCU)
	    Chest pain unit (CPU)
	Total time of preadmit process

Management of patients	# of chest pain admissions directly to CCU #/% of admissions directly to CCU ruled-in # of chest pain admissions directly to CCU discharged home from CCU within 24 hours of admission # of chest pain admissions to the CPU #/% of chest pain admission to CPU transferred to inpatient % transferred CPU patients ruled-in % of myocardial infarcts within six months of discharge from service #/% of deaths within six months of discharge from service % of cardiac deaths % of noncardiac deaths % of discharged patients returning to the emergency department with complaints of chest pain

* This is an illustrative, not a comprehensive, list of measures used for each project.

What Did Data Analysis Reveal?

A driving goal of the data analysis effort was to accurately understand performance while keeping the display formats and analysis techniques as simple as possible. The multidisciplinary improvement teams, with support and assistance from quality resource personnel, completed the data analyses. Basic descriptive statistical analysis used counts, averages, and ratios. These data were typically displayed on bar graphs, histograms, or pie charts. Nonstatistical approaches to data analysis included

- flowcharting, which helped to highlight key process steps requiring further study and/or improvement;
- thematic content analysis, which helped to identify recurrent performance patterns needing additional exploration; and
- affinity diagraming, which helped to cluster similar or related performance problems into common groups that became the target of further analysis and subsequent focus of improvement efforts.

Data analysis demonstrated the following:

1. Long lengths of inpatient stay:
   a. Average length of stay for cardiac catheterizations was 4.55 days, and
   b. Average length of stay for chest pain was 2.45 days.
2. Frequent clinic inaccessibility, including
   Scheduling backlogs:
   a. Average wait time for routine cardiology consultations was 45 days,
   b. Average wait time for urgent cardiology consultations was 5 days,
   c. Average wait time for routine echocardiograms was 90 days, and
   d. Average wait time for urgent echocardiograms was 5 days.

   Lengthy wait times (up to 4 weeks) from point of referral to first visit in the cardiology clinics.

   Limited availability of some clinic services, such as the Coumadin clinic, with weekday hours from 8:00 AM to 4:40 PM.
3. Complicated and lengthy (up to 6 hours) preadmission process for cardiac catheterizations.

4. Undesirable productivity:
   a. Total productivity was 2,500 patient contacts per month, and
   b. Productivity per provider was 95 patient contacts per month.
5. Fragmentation of cardiology services throughout the medical center and inadequate information transfer within the division.
6. Over-subspecialization of some technician and nursing staff.

How Did the Cardiology Services Improvement Project Improve Performance?

The examination of the Division of Cardiology's operations, resulting from this performance improvement initiative, revealed that the variety of available cardiology services was not coordinated across the medical center. Because this lack of coordination led to lost productivity and other operational inefficiencies and simultaneously compromised comprehensive, coordinated, and accessible cardiac care, it was recognized as a root cause of current performance. Once acknowledged, integration of the full spectrum of cardiology services became the driving improvement goal. To be successful, this service integration required a budget-neutral optimization of available resources. This was achieved by

1. re-emphasizing patient care and service as the primary priority of the division;
2. redefining staff responsibilities to focus on the direct provision of patient care and support of the care and treatment of patients; and
3. using cross-training to expand staff competencies to allow for flexible work assignments that respond to changing patient needs.

Stable clinical outcomes and improved operational and financial results have been the reward for staff efforts to creatively redefine and successfully implement more effective and efficient key processes. The specific improvements achieved in each of the three projects are summarized below.

Project #1: *Operations of the Cardiology Clinics and Noninvasive Laboratories*

Two compelling and interconnected patient-focused improvements relating to clinic and laboratory operations emerged from this project.

Administrators evaluated the tasks and responsibilities assigned to employed staff members and cardiology fellows. They discovered that many of their work activities did not have clinical components. As such, skilled practitioners were being directed away from clinical care. A re-emphasis on patient care and clinical services as the guiding mission of the cardiology division resulted in a major redefinition of the responsibilities of employed staff members and cardiology fellows. This freed them to spend significantly more time in direct patient care, which led to the following high-impact improvements that were financed through expense shifting and, therefore, resulted in no additional personnel-related costs.

1. The number of weekly half-day clinics doubled between 1995 (20) and 1997 (41). As a consequence, overall clinic productivity increased by 57% as illustrated in Figure 7-3, page 118.

2. By doubling the number of half-day clinic assignments for cardiology fellows (from 12 to 20) and tripling the number for employed staff members (from 10 to 32), clinic access time dramatically improved, as demonstrated in Figure 7-4, page 119.

By using patterns of patient volume to determine clinic staffing needs, more staff were scheduled during peak hours, less when patient flow was decreased. Because of this staffing model, Coumadin Clinic hours were expanded with no increase in personnel-related expenses.

Through cross-training, a clinic staff with highly subspecialized skills (for example, echocardiography, EKG, and so on) developed new and complementary competencies. Because individual staff now provide a variety of different services, the Division of Cardiology has maximized its overall capability to respond rapidly to patient needs.

Project #2: *Ratio between inpatient and outpatient cardiac catheterizations*

Several benefits resulted from dramatically reducing inpatient admissions for cardiac catheterizations. Patient satisfaction with pre-admission processes increased. Resource consumption decreased. Substantial cost savings were achieved. These improvements were accomplished without compromising patient outcomes.

The percent of outpatient cardiac catheterizations increased from 1% in 1995 to 58% in 1997. This shift to more outpatient cardiac catheterizations resulted in costs savings of approximately $3.6 million between 1995 and 1997. Interestingly, during this same time period the average length of stay for inpatient heart catheterizations dropped from 4.5 days to 1.5 days.

Same day admissions for all interventional cardiac catheterizations increased from 0% in 1995 to 60% in 1997, resulting in a cumulative cost savings of nearly $2.5 million. Interqual criteria were used to support this practice change, which did not negatively affect clinical outcomes. Patients now visit a preadmission clinic to prepare for their interventional cardiac catheterization. There, preprocedure testing is completed and patient education is provided. It is interesting to note that during this same time period the average length of stay for inpatient interventional heart catheterizations dropped from 6.5 days to slightly less than 3 days with no apparent deterioration in patient outcomes.

For uncomplicated cardioversion, the average length of stay was reduced from nearly 25 hours to 6.8 hours, with an average cost savings of $413 per procedure. No adverse effects occurred in relation to the shortened length of stay.

Traditionally, uncomplicated percutaneous transluminal angioplasty (PTCA) required a 3-day inpatient admission. It was shifted to a 24-hour, same-day procedure, with no untoward outcomes or decrease in patient satisfaction. An estimated cost savings of $4,411 per procedure has been realized.

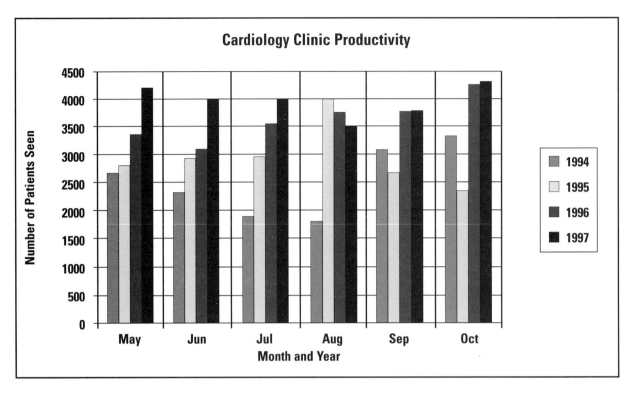

Figure 7-3. *This bar graph shows a 57% increase in cardiology clinic productivity, following role redefinition and increasing the number of half-day clinics.* **Source:** *Wilford-Hall Medical Center. Used with permission.*

In 1995, 100% of electrophysiology studies (EPS) were conducted as inpatient procedures. As of October 1997, 100% of all elective EPS admissions are scheduled as same-day procedures. No deleterious effects have been observed.

Project #3: *Management of patients with chest pain*

Historically, patients complaining of chest pain were admitted to a Coronary Care Unit (CCU) or Telemetry Unit. In some instances, admission to a critical area was clinically justified. At other times, patients could have been appropriately managed in a less intense level of service.

Benefits resulting from the initiation of a 24-hour chest pain observation unit (CPU) include the following:

1. Achievement of appropriate clinical outcomes. Of 731 admissions to the CPU,

   a. fourteen percent were newly diagnosed with coronary artery disease;

   b. nearly 3% experienced myocardial infarctions;

   c. nineteen percent were admitted to an inpatient service; and

   d. no patients died.

2. Better patient follow-up postprocedure. Each patient receives a telephone assessment 72 hours after discharge from the CPU.

3. More efficient use of medical center resources.

4. Decrease in inpatient census for patients complaining of chest pain, with a corresponding decrease in the number of inpatient beds from 12 to 6.

5. Cost savings of $12.5 million.

This divisionwide performance assessment and improvement effort generated the following additional process improvements:

- Eliminating voice mail for scheduling patient appointments;

- Scheduling follow-up appointments before the patient leaves the clinic;

- Introducing an urgent care provider into the clinic;

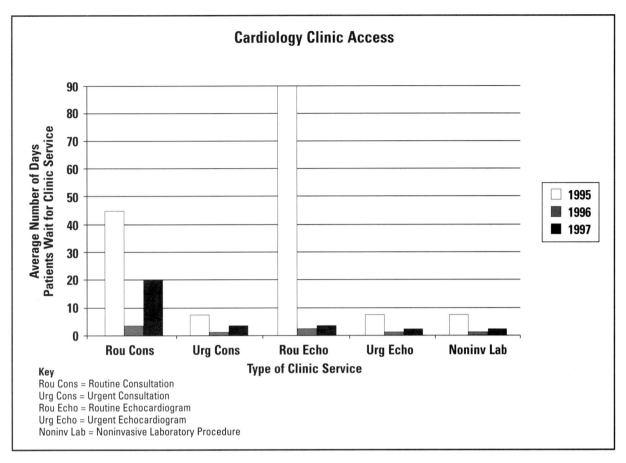

Cardiology Clinic Access

Key
Rou Cons = Routine Consultation
Urg Cons = Urgent Consultation
Rou Echo = Routine Echocardiogram
Urg Echo = Urgent Echocardiogram
Noninv Lab = Noninvasive Laboratory Procedure

Figure 7-4. *This bar graph illustrates the dramatic reduction in wait times for patients needing cardiology consultations, echocardiograms, and noninvasive procedures.* **Source:** *Wilford-Hall Medical Center. Used with permission.*

■ Instituting same-day admissions for all invasive procedures;

■ Creating a cardiology database and network;

■ Establishing Internet communications with referring physicians;

■ Initiating a 1-800 number for referring providers; and

■ Establishing a cardiology product line.

All health care organizations must balance the quality-cost equation. A comprehensive redesign of critical operational and patient care processes should produce better and/or maintain the current clinical outcomes. Simultaneously, process redesign should maximize the efficient use of time and other resources. Often these outcomes-oriented, process–focused improvements can save a health care organization millions of dollars. Figure 7-5, page 120, shows the changes in average, per patient, of diagnosis-related group (DRG) costs at WHMC. Between 1995 and 1997,

a net savings of $5.9 million in total DRG costs was appreciated.

Figure 7-6, page 120, illustrates overall patient satisfaction with the cardiology clinics at WHMC in comparison to key external benchmarks.

Lessons Learned

Wilford-Hall Medical Center learned six lessons as a result of their performance improvement projects:

1. A major paradigm shift is required in order to transition from inpatient treatment to outpatient care and same-day procedures. The success of the transition is predicated on demonstrating to physicians how resource use can be managed without compromising the quality of patient care.

2. Numerous logistic challenges accompany the creation of new service or care units. Geographic layout, required staffing,

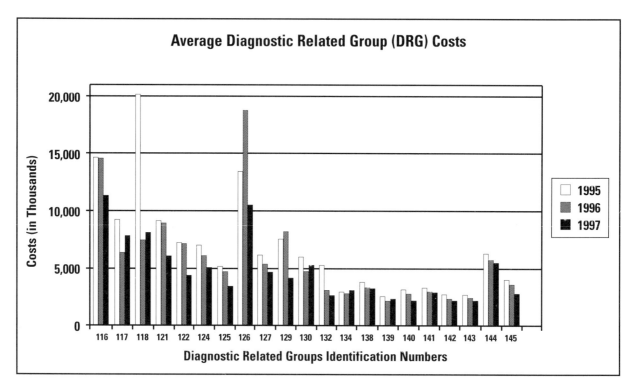

Figure 7-5. *This bar graph shows the average, per patient costs for selected diagnostic-related group.* **Source:** *Wilford-Hall Medical Center. Used with permission.*

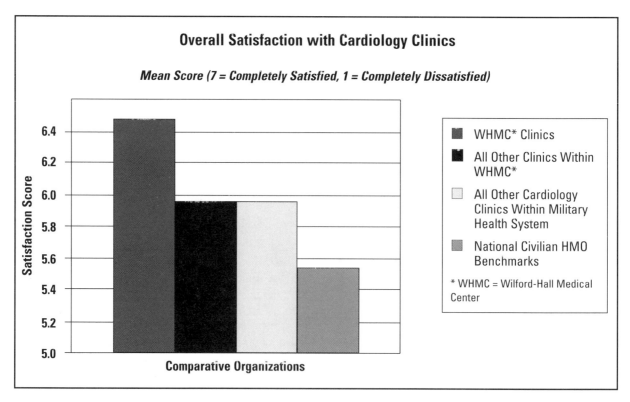

Figure 7-6. *This bar graph illustrates Wilford-Hall Medical Center cardiology patients' level of satisfaction with cardiology clinics. Wilford-Hall Performance is compared to standard Air Force benchmarks.* **Source:** *Wilford-Hall Medical Center. Used with permission.*

interfacing with other departments, and adhering to all internal and external requirements, standards, and guidelines pose potential problems that must be addressed.

3. A systematic performance measurement and improvement process that is implemented in a mission and values-driven culture characterized by empowerment, accountability, and support leads to the achievement of the desired goals and objectives.

4. It is important to continually move forward—never accepting the status quo, never becoming complacent always striving for excellence.

5. The experiences in improving the performance of the Division of Cardiology can be translated and used in other service units.

6. Remaining focused on the patients and their experiences with the care system is essential.

> **Case Story #2: The University of Massachusetts Memorial Health Care System: Easing the Pain**

What Is the University of Massachusetts Memorial Health Care System?

In 1976, the state of Massachusetts established the University of Massachusetts Memorial Health Care System (UMMHCS). The system exercises a strong influence on health care delivery throughout the state via its extensive satellite network of hospitals, clinics, and group practices.

As a tertiary care provider, UMMHCS offers the full spectrum of medical specialties and adjunctive clinical services across the continuum of care. Having recently undergone two mergers, it currently has more than 600 inpatient beds. Exceeding 600,000 visits in its ambulatory care sites each year, the UMMHCS is committed to providing primary health care services to a diverse community of individuals and families. A number of specialty clinics, such as the pain management clinic, offer services that augment primary care. Approximately 40% of patients seen within the system receive care under capitated, managed care contracts. Reflecting the aging of surrounding communities, increasingly more patients are Medicare recipients. As with most other academic health centers, patients receiving public entitlements and the indigent are also served.

The strategic driver for the evolution of UMMHCS is its **vision**, which states that the health care system "will be the leading provider of high-quality, comprehensive patient-centered health care within the academic setting, delivering the best value to our patients and other customers. We will be a central part of an integrated delivery system serving the Commonwealth and central New England."

The **mission** of UMMHCS is to serve the people of the Commonwealth through excellence in health sciences education, clinical care, research, and public service. Pursuit of mission achievement occurs in an organization climate that expects rigorous scientific inquiry, investigation,

and advancement. Through active living of their prized **values** of compassion, communication, consideration, access, respect, enthusiasm, diversity, fairness, objectivity, and social responsibility, all staff become personally accountable for creating an organization environment that optimizes the complementarity and contribution of the health care system's educative, clinical, research, and service components.

What Does Performance Improvement Mean at the University of Massachusetts Memorial Health Care System?

Continuous quality improvement at the UMMHCS is anchored in seven operating principles that link performance improvement with the organization's vision, mission, and values. These operating principles position the customer at the center of an integrated, interdependent organization system, powered by formal and informal teams. These teams champion openness, learning, and fact-based decision making in service of continuously streamlining process operations and achieving increasingly better outcomes.

The performance improvement program at UMMHCS revolves around 11 key objectives. It is particularly interesting to note that four of these objectives focus on measurement:

1. To institute a uniform measurement methodology that will streamline organization performance measurement;

2. To balance performance measurement so that it includes outcome measurement to understand results and process measurement to understand the cause of the results;

3. To design a well functioning performance improvement information management system that includes cost/resource utilization data, clinical and functional outcome data, and satisfaction level data from patients, families, care providers, and payers; and

4. To use comparative reference data bases as benchmarks for identifying performance improvement opportunities.

The performance improvement process at UMMHCS is grounded in the principles of process capability and stability, as first introduced by W. Edwards Deming. As such, all improvement efforts are aimed at

- determining performance targets or goals;
- achieving a data-based understanding of current performance;
- determining whether performance is stable or unstable;
- stabilizing unstable performance systems;
- comparing actual performance to desired performance;
- understanding the performance capability of each performance system;
- uncovering the causes of variation in achieved outcomes and operationalized processes;
- generating improvement theories;
- testing actions aimed at improving average performance and/or reducing variation;
- evaluating the outcome(s) of the test; and
- taking appropriate action based on the results of the test.

Two performance improvement methodologies are used at UMMHCS. A seven-step continuous quality improvement problem solving method was developed and implemented in 1990. This methodology is used when incremental improvement is needed; if the performance issue is being addressed at the worker, unit, or department level; and/or if the improvement goal is a 10%–20% gain. Figure 7-7, page 124, presents this methodology. In 1994, a seven-step redesign/re-engineering methodology was developed and implemented. This method is used if radical reorganization from current to ideal practice is needed, if senior management is involved and broad-based cross functional issues are being addressed, and/or if dramatic improvement is required with an improvement goal of 100%–300% gain. Figure 7-8, pages 125–126, presents this model.

What Is the Pain Management Service Improvement Project?

The Pain Management Service (PMS) at the UMMHCS is responsible for overseeing the comprehensive, multimodal management of pain experienced by hospitalized patients and those in ambulatory care settings. Each year,

approximately 3,000 inpatients and 10,000 outpatients receive pain management services. A pain management center is located in the medical center. Acute pain management is provided in each hospital as well as in three satellite clinics in Palmer, Milford, and Fitchburg, Massachusetts.

The Pain Management Service (PMS) began in 1976 and has been driven by a mission to provide quality pain management to all patients referred to the service. The infrastructure of the PMS (standards, policies, procedures, protocols, and tools) was created by the Manager of the Pain Service, Nancy Kowal, MS, RNC, NP, then reviewed and approved by the Medical Unit Chief, Donald Stevens, MD.

The pain management service is composed of a multidisciplinary team of professionals offering a variety of coordinated services throughout the health care system. These services include invasive pain management treatments; infusion/chemotherapy; psychological services; group therapy; biofeedback; physical, occupational, and speech therapies; acupuncture; wellness education and educational support; and health maintenance. Through a case management system, the pain management service provides individualized care and personalized pain tracking aimed at achieving defined goals and health outcomes.

Performance improvement efforts in the PMS always focus on facilitating the achievement of the best possible patient outcomes: maximal amelioration of pain, smallest effective dose of pain medications, maximal levels of activity, and maximal resolution of pain-related psychosocial issues. Standardized instruments used to assess a patient's current status include the

1. Acute Pain Survey Tool (adapted from the American Pain Society quality assurance standards for the relief of acute and cancer pain), a 12-item survey administered by the practitioner to assess the patient's overall current pain and pain management experience;

2. Quality of Life Scale (developed by Betty Ferrell, PhD, RN), completed by the patient, family, and the registered nurse, to

---

University of Massachusetts Memorial Health Care System
Seven-Step Continuous Quality Improvement Methodology

Step 1:   Determine the reason for improvement.
                   Are we meeting the customer expectations?
                   If not, what is the problem area?

Step 2:   Describe the current situation.
                   What is the problem and how bad is it?

Step 3:   Analyze causes.
                   What is the cause of the problem?

Step 4:   Identify potential solutions.
                   What can fix the cause of the problem?

Step 5:   Examine the results.
                   Did the fix work?
                   How well did it work?

Step 6:   Seek standardization.
                   Is the fix permanent?

Step 7:   Plan for the future.
                   What are the next steps?
                   How do we maintain the improvement that was made?

Figure 7-7. *This figure presents the seven-step continuous quality improvement process used at the University of Massachusetts Memorial Health Care System when conducting incremental improvement projects at the local level within the organization. Used with permission.*

assess four dimensions of care: psychological, physiological, social, and spiritual;

3. SF-36 (MOS 36-Item Short-Form Health Survey), a 36-item questionnaire that can be self-administered or administered by a practitioner to assess the patient's physical functioning, role functioning, bodily pain, social functioning, mental health, and vitality;

4. McGill Pain Questionnaire, a self-administered questionnaire using 20 sets of words that describe pain in order to scale pain in sensory, affective, and evaluative dimensions; and

5. Activity Tool, a self-administered assessment of the patient's activity levels for various specific activities.

Several performance improvement projects have been conducted in the PMS over the last few years, including

1. outcomes management in a pain management clinic;

2. factors affecting pain behaviors in surgical patients;

3. preprocedural education in a pain management clinic; and

4. evaluation of outcomes in a population of patients experiencing radicular low back pain (The Radicular Low Back Pain Improvement Project).

The fourth project will be explored in detail.

What Were the Goals of the Radicular Low Back Pain Improvement Project?

In considering a variety of prospective performance improvement projects, Ms. Kowal elected to initiate the Radicular Low Back Pain Improvement Project for the following reasons:

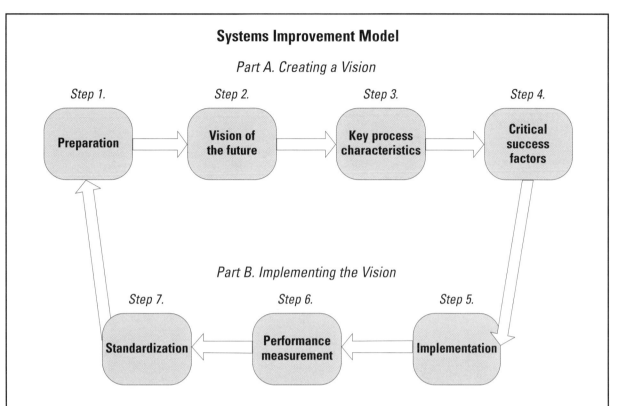

Systems Improvement Model

Part A. Creating a Vision

Step 1. Preparation → Step 2. Vision of the future → Step 3. Key process characteristics → Step 4. Critical success factors

Part B. Implementing the Vision

Step 7. Standardization ← Step 6. Performance measurement ← Step 5. Implementation

The following table describes the key activities to accomplish each step in the methodology.

Step	Activity
Preparation	1. Identify DRG, Chair, facilitator 2. Determine principal diagnoses/procedures and leader 3. Prepare an initial literature search 4. Confirm timeline, mutual expectations, resources, data sources 5. Describe System Improvement Team Structure 6. Review outcome benchmark data 7. Determine potential gains
Vision of the Future	1. Identify key stakeholders (Hint: those who are directly impacted or involved with the DRG or principle diagnoses/procedures) 2. Identify team members 3. Construct the macro flow for continuum of care 4. Define ideal care in terms of clinical outcomes, functional outcomes, patient satisfaction, and cost
Key Process Characteristics	1. Conduct a complete literature search 2. Determine internal/external issues and trends 3. Identify steps in the process 4. Measure clinical and functional outcomes, patient satisfaction, cost

continued on next page

Figure 7-8. *This figure presents the seven-step model used by the University of Massachusetts Memorial Health Care System for high impact, strategic improvements. Used with permission.*

Systems Improvement Model (continued)

Step	Activity
Critical Success Factors	1. Identify gaps between ideal and current situation. 2. Identify root cause barriers which are preventing the ideal. 3. Identify key decision points. 4. Identify non-value added steps.
Implementation Plan	1. Identify process steps: a. Need to be improved, b. Need to be redesigned, and c. Alternatives or contingencies. 2. Develop protocols to support process steps. 3. Present protocols to staff. 4. Finalize draft protocols. 5. Develop project plan for implementation. 6. Implement draft protocols. 7. Establish stretch goals.
Performance Measures	1. Continue to measure clinical and functional outcomes, patient satisfaction, and cost. 2. Measure variance from protocol. 3. Measure critical success factors. 4. Measure variation from benchmarks. 5. Measure remaining potential performance improvement.
Standardization	1. Analyze measurement information. 2. Modify protocol, if needed. 3. Educate Faculty, House Officers, nursing staff and others. 4. Confirm data sources, frequency, responsibility for monitoring and evaluation. 5. Implement plan. 6. Monitor key process characteristics and outcomes on a regular and periodic basis. 7. Incorporate M&E into House Officer, nursing staff and departmental education and JCAHO documentation. 8. Determine future plans which include feedback loops.

1. Radicular low back pain (RLBP) is a high-volume diagnosis (more than 60% of the population of patients with chronic pain have RLBP), especially in pain management centers.

2. RLBP is a high-cost diagnosis. (Costs include treatment costs, costs of lost work time, and disability-related costs.)

3. Effective management of RLBP is problem-prone.

4. Conservative management of RLBP includes physical therapy exercises and modalities, oral analgesics and anti-inflammatory medications, progressively increasing functional and social activities, and work hardening.

5. Enhancing conservative management with epidural steroid injections is an aggressive intervention for treating refractory RLBP.

6. Little clinical data demonstrate the outcomes achieved from conservative management or epidural steroid injections for patients with RLBP. This lack of data makes it difficult to select the best interventions.

A review of the descriptive database characterizing patients who were referred and treated for RLBP in UMMHCS Pain Management Service during the past two years revealed the following:

1. A total of 823 patients with RLBP were seen.

2. Thirty-eight percent (320) of RLBP patients were recipients of workers' compensation.

3. There was no case management for RLBP workers' compensation patients.

4. RLBP workers' compensation patients were in the health care system seven weeks longer than RLBP nonworkers' compensation patients. (Average length of treatment for all RLBP patients = 18 weeks, RLBP workers' compensation patients = 22 weeks, RLBP nonworkers' compensation patients = 15 weeks.)

Although it was not possible to calculate exact costs of care and other related costs in this study, it is apparent that the patients with RLBP receiving workers' compensation incurred higher costs than the comparison group. The workers' compensation RLBP patients were off work seven weeks longer and used more insurance resources than patients in the comparison group. Because of the increased costs for managing RLBP in patients on workers' compensation and Ms. Kowal's empirical experience working with such individuals, this group was selected as the sample of patients to be included in this improvement project.

Considering treatment approaches for RLBP and her chosen patient sample, Ms. Kowal theorized that the use of epidural steroid injections in patients with RLBP receiving workers' compensation would lead to a quicker resolution of symptoms and return to usual daily activities (including work).

Fundamentally, the RLBP improvement project tested this theory. Its specific goal was to compare clinical outcomes, cost, and quality of life in the RLBP workers' compensation patients treated with and without epidural steroid injections.

For the purposes of this study,

■ clinical outcomes included pain levels, pain medication use, activity levels, and psychosocial changes;

■ cost included average weekly wages, salary and benefits costs for temporary workers doing the RLBP patient's usual work, medical care costs, workers' compensation payments, costs related to insurance coverage, and administrative overhead; and

■ quality of life included psychological, physiological, social, and family issues and self-image.

What Data Were Collected?

Data were collected for 320 workers' compensation RLBP patients seen in the UMMHCS Pain Management Clinic between the beginning of 1995 through the end of 1996. Sixty-two percent of the group were male; 38% female. Patients' ages ranged from 22 to 80. The conservative group consisted of 185 patients treated without epidural steroid injections (ESI). The aggressive group included 135 patients treated with ESI.

A clinical record review produced information about patients'

1. pain level (0–10 scale),

2. pain medication usage,

3. activity levels, and

4. psychosocial changes.

Quality of life data were captured by data elements included in numbers 3 and 4, above. Average total costs were also calculated.

What Did Data Analysis Reveal?

Data analysis showed that aggressive treatment led to better outcomes in patients with RLBP who were receiving workers' compensation. These individuals had better pain control with fewer medications, improved activity capabilities, fewer lost work days, and a quicker return to work than their comparison group. In addition, slightly more than $1.5 million was saved by using aggressive treatment strategies. Table 7-2, page 128, compares the achieved outcomes between the conservatively and aggressively treated groups.

How Did the Radicular Low Back Pain Improvement Project Improve Performance?

This project has led to the development and use of a care model that achieves better patient

Table 7-2. Comparison of Achieved Outcomes Between the Conservatively and Aggressively Managed Groups

OUTCOME	CONSERVATIVE	AGGRESSIVE
1. Average pain level	8–10/10 pre Rx; 6–8/10 post Rx	8–10/10 pre ESI; 4–5/10 post ESI
2. Types of medications	NSAIDS, opioids, antidepressants, antiseizures	NSAIDS, opioids, antidepressants, muscle relaxants
3. Average medication dose	NSAIDS TID Opioids TID to qid Antidep. qd-TID at higher dose levels Mus. rel. BID to TID	NSAIDS BID-TID OPIOIDS BID-TID ANTIDEP. QD-TID MUS. REL. QHS
4. Average number of doses	4–6 daily	3–4 daily
5. Average dosing interval	Q6 hours	Q4–12 HOURS
6. Types of activity	Walking, resting, sleeping, bathing	Walking, water therapy, stress loading physical therapy, aerobics, and bicycling
7. Average number of activity changes	0–1	2
8. Average change in activity levels	1–2 more	4–6 more
9. Types of psychosocial changes	Weight loss, increased socialization, increased family interaction, smoking cessation	More positive self-image, weight reduction, increased socialization, smoking cessation
10. Average number of psychosocial changes	0–1	2–3
11. Average number of lost days of work	126	57
12. Average time to return to work	18 weeks	8 weeks
13. Average overall cost	$486,885	$324,590

outcomes with less resource consumption. This is, of course, the ultimate benefit of performance improvement.

Objective data demonstrated that epidural steroid injections (a more costly intervention than conservative interventions) led to several positive outcomes, including an overall reduction in treatment costs. As a result, reimbursement approvals have increased and denials have decreased. Before the study, approval rates ranged from 60% to 70%. After the study, reimbursement rates now exceed 98%.

The UMMHCS Pain Management Service plans to develop a practice guideline recommending the use of epidural steroid injections as an intervention that should be used earlier in the course of treatment for patients with RLBP.

The Pain Management Center hopes to develop an accepted practice standard that can be used to aid decision making on how to use and distribute health care services for patients with RLBP.

Because the UMMHCS Pain Management Service has demonstrated significant cost savings while simultaneously improving clinical outcomes through aggressive management of RLBP, it hopes to use these clinical and cost outcomes data to help negotiate and win managed care contracts.

Lessons Learned

Lessons learned by the UMMHCS Pain Management Service as a result of its radicular low back pain improvement project include the following:

1. Providing a "quality" pain management service will lead to the achievement of "quality" outcomes in patients with pain.

2. Combining epidural steroid injections with physical therapy and pain medication results in the best patient outcomes.

3. Ambulatory care centers and other provider organizations should explore ways to track costs of care more effectively and efficiently.

APPENDIX

WORKSHEETS

The worksheets in this Appendix offer a structured approach to clarifying and conducting performance measurement initiatives in practice environments. They can also help organizations develop their own outcomes measurement program.

Worksheet #1. Types of Performance Measures

PART I. Definitions

Provide a definition that is meaningful in your own ambulatory care organization for each of the three types of performance measures.

STRUCTURE MEASURES: _____

_____

_____

_____

_____

PROCESS MEASURES: _____

_____

_____

_____

_____

OUTCOMES MEASURES: _____

_____

_____

_____

_____

PART II. Structures, Processes, and Outcomes: Ambulatory Examples

Provide at least three examples each of key structures, processes, and outcomes present in your ambulatory care setting.

STRUCTURES:_____

_____

_____

_____

_____

PROCESSES:_____

_____

_____

_____

_____

OUTCOMES: _____

_____

_____

_____

_____

Worksheet #2. Reviewing the Effectiveness of Performance Measurement

This worksheet can be used to examine the effectiveness of performance measurement in your ambulatory care organization. You may evaluate performance measurement efforts at the level of the organization as a whole, or at any discrete level within the organization (for example, individual departments or specific measurement/improvement projects).

PART I.   Assessing the Effectiveness of Measurement

Down the left side of the following grid, list the measurement initiative(s) you are interested in reviewing. Then evaluate each initiative in relation to each characteristic of effective performance measurement identified at the top of the grid. Using a Y for Yes and an N for No, record in each corresponding grid cell whether a measurement project successfully achieves each effectiveness characteristic. Once you have completed the grid, analyze the patterns of Ys and Ns to determine if a specific measurement effort meets all or most of the effectiveness traits. If a measurement project appears to be ineffective, circle it and complete Part II of this worksheet.

Specific Measurement Effort	Effectiveness Characteristics						
	R	V	RLVT	C	VTION	U	CE

Effectiveness Characteristic Key:

R = Reliable	V = Valid	RLVT = Relevant
C = Comprehensive	VTION = Reveals Variation	
U = Useful	CE = Cost-effective	

PART II.   Addressing Ineffective Measurement

List each of your ineffective measurement initiatives down the left side of the following grid. Use a check mark to specify what will be done to address them. Consider reassessing effectiveness characteristics of the ineffective measurement initiatives to rule out any error(s) in the way you may have evaluated the measure; revise the measurement effort to strengthen it; or eliminate it.

Ineffective Measurement	Re-assess	Revise	Eliminate

continued on next page

Worksheet #2. Reviewing the Effectiveness of Performance Measurement (continued)

PART III. Developing A Plan To Address Selected Ineffective Measurement Initiatives

Use the following guidelines to strengthen the effectiveness characteristics for those measurement initiatives you decided to revise (as recorded in Part II). Then complete the following action plan, specifying how you will improve your selected ineffective measurement initiatives.

Guidelines

If You Want To Improve: *Consider The Following:*

Reliability

Review the measure to be sure it will collect the same data over time (that is, that data collectors will always abstract and record the data in the same way). Review the measure to ensure that different data collectors will record the data in the same way. To improve reliability, restate the measure as clearly, concretely, and completely as possible. Train data collectors so that abstracting and recording of data will be consistent. Pilot test the measure to determine if it consistently collects the data it is intended to collect. Be sure to review the data for consistency over time and across data collectors.

Validity

Check with content experts, clinical guidelines, and professional literature to be sure the measure is an appropriate assessment for the issue of interest. To improve validity, review carefully, in as much detail as possible, what you want to know. Then consider whether this measure will provide that information. Ask yourself if the measure makes sense for the issue under consideration. Review how others have elicited information that is the same or similar to what you are seeking. Pilot test the measure to see if you accurately acquire the needed data at the necessary degree of detail.

Relevance

Review your organization's strategic goals and high-priority/high impact areas. Consider where resources have or will be dedicated. Ask yourself how pertinent this measurement activity is to the critical areas of your organization's performance. To improve relevance, realign your measurement efforts with the strategic plan and goals. Goals may call for maintenance of current activities, improvement of existing activities, or initiation of new activities. Ask data users if they will find the information derived from this initiative to be helpful. Will it tell them something they need/want to know?

Comprehensiveness

Think about the measurement/improvement issue of concern. Determine if the measurement component will produce data for all aspects of the issue. If it does not, identify the missing areas. Decide whether you should include those areas. Determine if any information that is essential for decision making is lacking. If so, how can you acquire that information? Evaluate how valuable this measurement effort is to data users. Are there ways it could be made more valuable? Would increasing its scope enhance its value by making it more comprehensive? To improve comprehensiveness, list all the critical data and information needs identified by the data users. Check to see if the measurement effort addresses all these areas. Develop additional measures that address the gaps you identified. Conduct a pilot test. Collect data and then present findings to data customers. Ask them to critique what they have received to determine if it includes all the information they need to know about this issue. If it does not, assist them to clarify their

continued on next page

Worksheet #2. Reviewing the Effectiveness of Performance Measurement (continued)

data/information needs in as much detail as possible. Then, generate and test additional measures. With data users, evaluate whether this new combination of measures more comprehensively produces the data and information that is required.

Reveals Variation

Recall that a performance improvement effort always examines achieved performance against another critical variable of interest. Typically this variable is time. However, it may be different organizations, subunits of different organizations, subunits within a single organization, or different classes, categories, or individuals. Remember that process performance and achieved results always vary to some degree. Therefore, you can always expect to see a performance range; a highest (largest) value or data point; a lowest (smallest) value or data point; multiple values or data points between the highest and lowest; and a performance average. Review how you plan to calculate average performance. Will you use a mean or median? Ranges, standard deviations, line graphs, and control charts may be used to reveal variance in performance. Which of these approaches will you use in this measurement effort? Remember it is essential to have a large enough number of data points to achieve an accurate understanding of the degree of variance that is present. Typically, no fewer than 15 to 20 data points should be used. How many data points do you plan to have before you begin to look at the variance that is present? To improve the revelation of variance, examine your measures to be sure they assess actual performance against some other important variable. Talk with the data users and then identify what that variable is and define it as clearly as possible. Ask them how they want to understand the performance variability. Do they want a simple illustration of the variability? If so, consider using the mean, median, or line graph. Do they want a description of the magnitude of the variability? If so, consider using the standard deviation. Do they want to determine what kinds of actions to take to respond to the existing variation? If so, consider using control charts. Decide what tactic(s) you will use to demonstrate the variance. Then, conduct a pilot test. Use your measure to collect at least 15 data points. Apply your selected approach to demonstrating variance. Ask yourself if it addresses the measurement purposes your data users specified. Show the data customers results of your pilot. Ask them if it gives them the information they need. Sometimes the pilot test will clarify the reasons for examining variance. Often, it will be necessary to decide to use another or a different approach for revealing variation. Be prepared to recommend such an approach.

Usefulness

Remember that the usefulness of performance measurement is a combination of its relevance and the ability to take action based on the performance data/information that is generated. Consider your measurement effort. Have you maximized its relevance? Will the findings of your initiative be practical and applicable to the "real world" of your organization? Determine if you are presenting the measurement results in an easy to understand, actionable format. To improve usefulness, review the measures and data elements with data users to determine if this measurement will meet their information needs. Ask them if it will provide an

continued on next page

Worksheet #2. Reviewing the Effectiveness of Performance Measurement (continued)

illustration of performance that they can use as a guide for implementing corrective or improvement actions. Pilot test the measures. Then, work with data customers to simulate an improvement activity. In that simulation identify any factors that reduce or fail to contribute to the usability and usefulness of the measures or data they collect. Modify those factors and pilot again to test the changes that were made.

Cost-Effectiveness   To determine cost-effectiveness of the measurement effort, simulate a data collection, analysis, and performance improvement activity. Attach costs to these activities. Consider costs such as staff salary and time, any needed equipment or supplies, any consultant/consultation fees. Next, identify the expected gains from this effort. Consider reduced costs for process operations, time savings, increased revenue, improved customer satisfaction. Examine the relationship of the costs to the benefits. Determine if this is an acceptable or desirable ratio. To improve cost-effectiveness align performance measurement initiatives with high-impact, high-cost, high volume, high-risk, and problem prone areas. Try to keep the measurement component of the improvement effort as inexpensive as you possibly can, while still maintaining the integrity of the measurement. This will spare finite resources for the implementation of improvement actions.

Action Plan for Strengthening Selected Measurement Efforts

Measurement Effort	What Will Be Done to Improve?	Who Will Make the Improvements?	Start/End Dates

Worksheet #3. Assessment of Stakeholder's Outcomes Data/Information Needs

PART I. Identify and list all key internal and external stakeholders who need outcomes data/information from you.

1._____   6. _____

2._____   7. _____

3._____   8. _____

4._____   9. _____

5._____   10. _____

PART II. Interview each stakeholder identified above to discover key facts about the specific data and information they need. Use the following questions as the framework for the interview.

NAME OF STAKEHOLDER: _____

1. What types of *information* about this organization (or project) do you need? _____

_____

_____

_____

2. Why do you need and how do you use such *information*?

INFORMATION	WHY NEEDED	HOW USED

3. What types of *data* about this organization (or project) do you need? _____

_____

_____

_____

a. Do you need *patient demographic data?*   YES   NO
   If yes, specifically describe the data you need, including the period of time for which you need to see the data. _____

   _____

   _____

b. Do you need *clinical outcomes data?*   YES   NO
   If yes, specifically describe the data you need, including the period of time for which you need to see the data. _____

   _____

   _____

c. Do you need *financial outcomes data?*   YES   NO
   If yes, specifically describe the data you need, including the period of time for which you need to see the data. _____

   _____

   _____

continued on next page

Worksheet #3. Assessment of Stakeholder's Outcomes Data/Information Needs (continued)

d. Do you need other *outcomes data?*   YES   NO
(If yes, specify.) _____
_____
_____

4. How do you need such outcomes *data* categorized?
(Circle the type of categorization that the stakeholder needs for each data type. One type of data may need to be categorized in more than one way.)

DATA TYPE	CATEGORIZATION
Demographic (for example, patient diagnosis, age, referral source, and so on)	By diagnosis? By type of service? By type of intervention? By payer source?
Clinical outcomes (for example, patient disposition, change in condition, self-care status, and so on)	By diagnosis? By type of service? By type of intervention?
Financial outcomes	By diagnosis? By type of service? By type of intervention? By payer source? Overall financial performance (for example, profit and loss, net revenue, and so on)?
Other (specify)	_____ _____ _____

5. What are your issues related to severity-adjustment of data? _____
_____
_____
_____

6. What types of *information* about this organization's staff and licensed independent practitioners (LIPs) do you need? _____
_____
_____
_____

7. Why do you need and how do you use such *information?*

INFORMATION	WHY NEEDED	HOW USED
_____	_____	_____
_____	_____	_____
_____	_____	_____
_____	_____	_____
_____	_____	_____
_____	_____	_____
_____	_____	_____

continued on next page

Worksheet #3. Assessment of Stakeholder's Outcomes Data/Information Needs (continued)

8. What types of *data* about staff and LIPs do you need? _____
_____
_____
_____

   a. Do you need *staff and practitioner demographic data?*   YES   NO
      If yes, specifically describe the data you need, including the period of time for which
      you need to see the data. _____
        _____
        _____

   b. Do you need *staff and practitioner number/mix data?*   YES   NO
      If yes, specifically describe the data you need, including the period for which you
      need to see the data._____
        _____
        _____

   c. Do you need *staff and practitioner competency data?*   YES   NO
      If yes, specifically describe the data you need, including the period of time for which
      you need to see the data. _____
        _____
        _____

9. How do you need the data/information presented?

NEEDED DATA/INFORMATION	PRESENTATION	
	Graphical/Tabular	Narrative Summaries
_____	_____	_____
_____	_____	_____
_____	_____	_____
_____	_____	_____
_____	_____	_____
_____	_____	_____

10. How frequently do you need data/information reports?

DATA/INFORMATION REPORT	FREQUENCY OF REPORT
_____	_____
_____	_____
_____	_____
_____	_____
_____	_____

Worksheet #4. Determining Areas for Organization Improvement

1. Identify and *briefly* describe your organization's **core** clinical processes. (Consider such things as admission, assessment and reassessment, identification of problems and goals, initiating and revising treatment plans, and providing interventions.)_____
   _____
   _____
   _____

2. Review the following list and circle those items that are **high volume** at your organization.
   Age-based patient population:
   - ❏ Children
   - ❏ Adolescents
   - ❏ Adults (younger than 65)
   - ❏ Older adults (65+)

   Diagnosis-based patient population: *Patients with problems of the following body systems:*
   - ❏ Cardiac
   - ❏ Endocrine
   - ❏ Gastrointestinal
   - ❏ Genitourinary
   - ❏ Integumentary
   - ❏ Mental/psychological
   - ❏ Musculoskeletal
   - ❏ Neurologic
   - ❏ Pulmonary
   - ❏ Renal
   - ❏ Vascular

   Clinical Services:
   - ❏ Chiropractic
   - ❏ Dental
   - ❏ Diagnostic studies
   - ❏ Medical
   - ❏ Nursing
   - ❏ Rehabilitation
   - ❏ Surgical
   - ❏ Other (specify): _____

   Interventional strategies:
   - ❏ Ambulatory surgery
   - ❏ Dialysis
   - ❏ Endoscopy
   - ❏ Infusion therapy
   - ❏ Invasive cardiology
   - ❏ Labor and delivery
   - ❏ Laser treatments
   - ❏ Lithotripsy
   - ❏ Medication management
   - ❏ Ophthalmologic surgery
   - ❏ Patient education
   - ❏ Pain control/management
   - ❏ Physical therapy
   - ❏ Plastic surgery
   - ❏ Podiatric services
   - ❏ Radiation therapy
   - ❏ Sleep studies
   - ❏ Other (specify): _____

3. Review the following list and circle those items that are **high risk** at your organization.
   Symptom-based patient population: *Patients with:*
   - ❏ High risk pregnancy
   - ❏ Impaired immunity
   - ❏ Infectious processes
   - ❏ Multi-system impairment
   - ❏ Pain
   - ❏ Substance abuse
   - ❏ Other (specify): _____

   Therapeutic modalities:
   - ❏ Infusion therapy
   - ❏ Laser
   - ❏ Pharmacotherapy
   - ❏ Radiation therapy
   - ❏ Surgery
   - ❏ Other (specify): _____

   Specific treatments:
   - ❏ IV cancer chemotherapy
   - ❏ Investigational pharmacotherapy
   - ❏ Investigational treatments
   - ❏ Other (specify): _____

continued on next page

Worksheet #4. Determining Areas for Organization Improvement (continued)

Sentinel events:
Adverse clinical events (for example, missed diagnosis, misdiagnosis, tissue destruction due to vesicant extravasation, surgical mishaps, complications from anesthesia or sedation, complications of labor or delivery, unexpected deaths, and so on)

Other:
❏ Anesthesia   ❏ Sedation
❏ Impaired literacy   ❏ Other (specify): _____
❏ Low socioeconomic status

4. Review the following list and circle those items that are **problem prone** at your organization.
   Diagnosis-based patient population:
   ❏ AIDS   ❏ Malnutrition
   ❏ Cancer   ❏ STDs
   ❏ Chronic pain syndromes   ❏ Substance abuse
   ❏ Diabetes mellitus   ❏ Tuberculosis
   ❏ Headache   ❏ Other (specify): _____

   Therapeutic modalities:
   ❏ Lifestyle modification   ❏ Patient education
   ❏ Nutritional management   ❏ Pharmacotherapy
   ❏ Pain management   ❏ Other (specify): _____

   Specific treatments:
   ❏ Behavior modification   ❏ Self-medication
   ❏ Dietary modification   ❏ Self-monitoring (blood pressure, blood
   ❏ Physical exercise   sugar, and so on)
                                        ❏ Other (specify): _____

5. Review the following list and circle those items that are **high cost** at your organization.
   Therapeutic modalities:
   ❏ Laser   ❏ Radiation
   ❏ Medical management/monitoring   ❏ Surgery
   ❏ Pharmacotherapy   ❏ Other (specify): _____

   Specific treatments (Specify):
   ❏ _____   ❏ _____
   ❏ _____   ❏ _____
   ❏ _____   ❏ _____

   Other:
   ❏ Anesthesia   ❏ Other (specify): _____

6. Identify and *briefly* describe your organization's **core** operations processes. (Consider such things as referral, registration, resource/service utilization, continuity of care, quality control, and documentation and record keeping.) _____
   _____
   _____
   _____

continued on next page

Worksheet #4. Determining Areas for Organization Improvement (continued)

7. Identify and *briefly* describe your organization's **core** administrative processes. (Consider such things as staffing ratios; staff mix; staff competency; staff perceptions of improvement opportunities; integration of clinical, operational, administrative, and support services; community relations; patient satisfaction; staff safety; billing; and financial performance.) _____

_____

_____

_____

8. Which of the issues identified in questions 1–7 are strongly related to your organization's current mission and future vision? _____

_____

_____

_____

9. Which of the issues identified in questions 1–7 are strongly related to your organization's current strategic, improvement, and operational plans? _____

_____

_____

_____

10. Which of the issues identified in questions 1–7 are strongly related to known needs of your patients? _____

_____

_____

_____

11. In which of the issues identified in questions 8–10 do performance data demonstrate a clear and present need for improvement? _____

_____

_____

_____

    a. Why must each of these issues be improved? _____

       _____

       _____

    b. What specific risks are associated with failing to improve each of these issues?_____

       _____

       _____

    c. What resources will be needed to improve each of these issues? _____

       _____

       _____

    d. What is the "improvement urgency rating" for each issue requiring improvement (1 = not at all urgent; 3 = urgent; 5 = extremely urgent)? _____

       _____

       _____

12. In which of the issues identified in questions 8–10 do performance data demonstrate acceptable performance? _____

_____

_____

_____

continued on next page

Worksheet #4. Determining Areas for Organization Improvement (continued)

    a. Is there a need to improve any of these issues that demonstrate acceptable performance? If yes, specify why. _____
_____
_____

    b. What specific risks are associated with failing to improve each issue? _____
_____
_____

    c. What resources will be needed to improve each issue? _____
_____

    d. What is the "improvement urgency rating" for each issue requiring improvement (1 = not at all urgent; 3 = urgent; 5 = extremely urgent)? _____
_____
_____

    e. Is there a goal to maintain the current performance level of any of these issues that demonstrate acceptable performance? If yes, specify why. _____
_____
_____

13. Are there any priorities identified in the mission or vision statement, strategic, performance improvement, or operational plans, or definition of patient needs for which no performance data are available?_____
_____
_____
_____

    a. If not, why not? _____
_____

    b. Should such performance data be obtained? Why or why not? _____
_____
_____

    c. Who will be responsible for collecting those data?_____
_____
_____

14. Analyze your responses to the previous 13 questions. Then, generate a rank-ordered list of potential improvement initiatives for your organization, beginning with the most important/highest impact improvement opportunity. _____
_____
_____
_____

Worksheet #5. Assessing Organization Commitment to Performance Measurement and Improvement

Place a check mark in the column indicating the most appropriate response to each of the following questions. The greater the number of yes responses, the more committed your organization is to performance measurement and improvement.

QUESTION	YES	NO	NOT SURE
In your organization at this time:			
Top leadership:			
1. Serves as the official oversight body for performance measurement and improvement.			
2. Communicates the value and importance of performance measurement and improvement throughout the organization.			
3. Strives to build effective organization relationships with all vested stakeholders.			
4. Demands the active solicitation of stakeholders' data, information, and service needs.			
5. Establishes and communicates organization improvement priorities.			
6. Selects and supports the implementation of a manageable number of high-impact improvement projects.			
7. Mandates the development and use of organizationwide performance improvement protocols.			
8. Requires the development and implementation of a performance measurement and improvement plan that is aligned with the organization's strategic goals and objectives.			
9. Endorses and requires the use of a single performance improvement method across the organization.			
10. Role models the use of performance measurement and improvement tools and techniques.			
11. Role models databased decision making.			
12. Manages by asking questions that require staff to collect, interpret, and use performance data.			
13. Allocates essential performance measurement and improvement resources, such as Personnel: Education/training: Time: Technological support:			
14. Has required the inclusion of staff competencies related to performance measurement and improvement in Job descriptions:			
Performance appraisals:			
Recruitment and promotion interviews:			

continued on next page

Worksheet #5. Assessing Organization Commitment to Performance Measurement and Improvement (continued)

QUESTION	YES	NO	NOT SURE
15. Routinely acknowledges performance measurement and improvement successes and efforts: Publicly:			
Privately:			
16. Does not allow disciplinary or punitive actions to be based on performance measurement or improvement efforts.			
17. Systematically assesses the effectiveness of the organization's performance improvement methodology.			
18. Routinely assesses the effectiveness of the organization's performance improvement process.			
Staff: 19. Understand the organization's mission, vision, values, and strategic goals and objectives.			
20. Understand how their own work contributes to the successful accomplishment of the organization's mission, vision, values, and strategic goals and objectives.			
21. Are familiar with the organization's performance measurement and improvement plan.			
22. Understand their own role in organization performance measurement and improvement.			
23. Directly and indirectly support the organization's achievement of its performance improvement priorities.			
24. Are knowledgeable about the organization's Performance improvement method:			
Performance measurement:			
Performance improvement tools:			
25. Adhere to the organization's established performance measurement and improvement protocols.			
26. Routinely participate in performance improvement-related education: General inservices:			
Just-in-time education:			
27. View performance measurement and improvement as a core part of their daily work.			
28. Routinely use the organization's chosen improvement method to measure, assess, and improve their own work processes and outcomes.			
29. Use the organization's chosen improvement method while participating in assigned performance improvement projects.			

continued on next page

Worksheet #5. Assessing Organization Commitment to Performance Measurement and Improvement (continued)

QUESTION	YES	NO	NOT SURE
30. Focus on understanding the needs of Their immediate customers: The organization's customers:			
31. Strive to build effective working relationships with all customers.			
32. Demonstrate databased decision making.			

Worksheet #6. Examples of Performance Measures

PART I. **Clinical outcomes measures**

For each of the specified health domains, develop at least three outcomes measures that could be used at your ambulatory care organization.

DOMAIN: HEALTH STATUS

1. _____

2. _____

3. _____

DOMAIN: FUNCTIONALITY

1. _____

2. _____

3. _____

DOMAIN: WELL-BEING

1. _____

2. _____

3. _____

DOMAIN: QUALITY OF LIFE

1. _____

2. _____

3. _____

PART II. **Nonclinical outcomes measures**

For each of the specified performance dimensions, develop at least three administrative or operational (nonclinical) outcomes measures that could be used at your ambulatory care organization.

DIMENSION: AVAILABILITY

1. _____

2. _____

3. _____

continued on next page

Worksheet #6. Examples of Performance Measures (continued)

DIMENSION: TIMELINESS

1. _____

_____

2. _____

_____

3. _____

_____

DIMENSION: EFFECTIVENESS

1. _____

_____

2. _____

_____

3. _____

_____

DIMENSION: CONTINUITY

1. _____

_____

2. _____

_____

3. _____

_____

DIMENSION: SAFETY

1. _____

_____

2. _____

_____

3. _____

_____

DIMENSION: EFFICIENCY

1. _____

_____

2. _____

_____

3. _____

_____

PART III. **Patient perception of care and services (satisfaction) measures**
For each of the specified areas of patient perception (APP), develop at least three patient-focused satisfaction measures that could be used at your ambulatory care organization.

APP: CARE PROCESSES EXPERIENCED IN AN EPISODE OF CARE

1. _____

_____

2. _____

_____

3. _____

_____

continued on next page

Worksheet #6. Examples of Performance Measures (continued)

APP: HEALTH BENEFITS RESULTING FROM THE EPISODE OF CARE

1. _____

2. _____

3. _____

APP: VALUE OF THE EPISODE OF CARE

1. _____

2. _____

3. _____

APP: GLOBAL HEALTH CARE EXPERIENCE

1. _____

2. _____

3. _____

APP: OVERALL QUALITY OF THE AMBULATORY CARE ORGANIZATION

1. _____

2. _____

3. _____

PART IV. Financial measures

For each of the specified economic categories, develop at least three financial measures that could be used at your ambulatory care organization.

CATEGORY: RESOURCE CONSUMPTION

1. _____

2. _____

3. _____

CATEGORY: CHARGES

1. _____

2. _____

3. _____

continued on next page

Worksheet #6. Examples of Performance Measures (continued)

CATEGORY: **COSTS**

1. _____
   _____

2. _____
   _____

3. _____
   _____

CATEGORY: **GLOBAL FINANCIAL PERFORMANCE**

1. _____
   _____

2. _____
   _____

3. _____
   _____

Worksheet #7. Action Plan for Evaluating and Selecting a Performance Measurement System

Consider specifically what needs to be done to evaluate and select a performance measurement system for use in your organization. Think about the overall goal and final "deliverables" of this evaluation and selection process. Identify any critical internal or external deadlines. List detailed action steps that must be taken to successfully identify, evaluate, and select a performance measurement system that is compatible with your organization's needs. Specify who needs to be involved and in what capacity. Determine due dates that help you meet established deadlines. Document your detailed action plan using the following format, which includes the eight major action steps that must be taken.

Performance Measurement System Selection: Action Plan

Project Title: Project Deadline:

Project Goal: Deliverable(s):

ACTION STEP	RESPONSIBLE PARTY	DUE DATE
1. Identify your organization's measurement goals.		
2. Establish a clear and objective evaluation process.		
3. Evaluate systems using selection criteria.		
4. Use a selection grid or checklist to facilitate comparison of the different systems.		

continued on next page

Worksheet #7. Action Plan for Evaluating and Selecting a Performance Measurement System (continued)

ACTION STEP	RESPONSIBLE PARTY	DUE DATE
5. Review the list of acceptable systems and develop a "short list."		
6. Narrow your "short list" to a final list.		
7. Check customer references for each system on your final list.		
8. Select the system(s) that seem most appropriate for your organization.		

Worksheet #8. Designing an Outcomes-based Performance Improvement Project

Improvement Project Title: _____

Improvement Team Composition:

Team Role	Name	Title	Work Unit
Executive sponsor:	_____	_____	_____
Leader:	_____	_____	_____
Facilitator:	_____	_____	_____
Data consultant:	_____	_____	_____
Members:	_____	_____	_____
(specify if ad hoc)	_____	_____	_____
	_____	_____	_____
	_____	_____	_____
	_____	_____	_____
	_____	_____	_____

Improvement Project Rationale: Briefly describe the reasons for conducting this outcomes-based performance improvement project. Specify any current problems or issues that highlighted the need for this project. Cite any pertinent related performance data. Relate this issue to the organization's mission, vision, strategic goals and objectives, and/or improvement priorities.

_____
_____
_____
_____

Improvement Project Goal(s): Describe the aim of this outcomes-based performance improvement project. List all the expected/desired benefits of this project. Identify any specific end products or "deliverables" that will result from this project (such as new protocols, procedures, processes, policies, forms, and so forth).

_____
_____
_____
_____

Improvement Project Scope: Define the boundaries of this outcomes-based improvement project. Detail what functions, processes, outcomes, patient populations, and work areas will be included in and excluded from this project. Briefly explain the reasons for inclusion and exclusion.

_____
_____
_____
_____

Anticipated Resources: Consider the goals and scope of this outcomes-based performance improvement project. Then specify the resources you think you will need to successfully complete this project. Such resources might include consulting, benchmarking, continuing education, technological support, and so forth.

_____
_____
_____
_____

continued on next page

Worksheet #8. Designing an Outcomes-based Performance Improvement Project (continued)

Improvement Project Success Measures: Specify a few high level measures that will demonstrate this outcomes-based improvement project's success. Develop at least two measures each for patient outcomes (for example, improved functional capacity or increased satisfaction), organization outcomes (for example, decreased organization risk or improved financial performance), operational processes (for example, reductions in process variations or improved process capability), and resource consumption (reduction of rework or appropriate staffing).

_____

_____

_____

_____

Improvement Project Constraints: Determine any specific limitations or requirements related to the work of the outcomes-based performance improvement team itself or the recommended improvements. Document budgetary constraints; project deadlines and time lines for instituting improvements; and any limitations on the type, number, or nature of the improvement recommendations.

_____

_____

_____

_____

Anticipated Problems: Identify any issues or concerns about the planning, implementation, and evaluation of this outcomes-based performance improvement project. Think about possible hidden agendas and potential political or turf issues.

_____

_____

_____

_____

Improvement Project Time Line with Key Milestones: Indicate when each of the following key milestones will be met.

First team meeting will occur on: _____

Data collection will begin on: _____

Data collection will be complete on: _____

Data analysis will begin on: _____

Data analysis will be complete on: _____

Root cause analysis will begin on: _____

Root cause analysis will be complete on: _____

Generation of improvement recommendations will be complete on: _____

Final report with recommendations will be complete on: _____

Improvement Project Reporting Protocol: Circle the most appropriate response to the following six items.

1. Intermediate project reports will be:
   ❏ WRITTEN   ❏ ORAL   ❏ BOTH

2. Intermediate project reports will be given by the:
   ❏ TEAM   ❏ TEAM   ❏ LEADER

3. Intermediate project reports will be given to:
   ❏ QUALITY OVERSIGHT GROUP   ❏ SPONSOR   ❏ BOTH

continued on next page

Worksheet #8. Designing an Outcomes-based Performance Improvement Project (continued)

4. Final project report will be:
   ❏ WRITTEN   ❏ ORAL   ❏ BOTH

5. Final project report will be given by:
   ❏ TEAM   ❏ TEAM   ❏ LEADER

6. Final project report will be given to:
   ❏ QUALITY OVERSIGHT GROUP   ❏ SPONSOR   ❏ BOTH

Worksheet #9. Data Management Plan

PART I.   Preparing For Data Collection

1. Briefly summarize the purpose of the outcomes-based improvement project. _____
   _____
   _____
   _____

2. Specify the project sample.
   a. Determine the population of interest (for example, age, gender, diagnosis, treatment setting, and so forth). _____
      _____
      _____

   b. Define the study sample (for example, sample size, sampling strategy, inclusion/exclusion criteria, and so forth). _____
      _____
      _____

   c. Identify any limitations related to the sample (for example, size, lack of generalizability, inherent bias, and so forth). _____
      _____
      _____

3. Determine data needs.
   a. Detail the information necessary to accomplish the study purpose. _____
      _____
      _____

   b. Fill in the table below to
      - create a comprehensive list of the data needed to produce such information;
      - document indicators (you may adopt or adapt existing indicators or develop new indicators);
      - define the data elements for each indicator; and
      - determine data sources.

NEEDED DATA	INDICATOR	DATA ELEMENT DEFINITIONS	SOURCE
_____	_____	_____	_____
_____	_____	_____	_____
_____	_____	_____	_____
_____	_____	_____	_____
_____	_____	_____	_____
_____	_____	_____	_____
_____	_____	_____	_____
_____	_____	_____	_____
_____	_____	_____	_____
_____	_____	_____	_____
_____	_____	_____	_____

4. Create the data collection tool. Include the following on the tool:
   - Indicators with any pertinent data element definitions;
   - Data source for each indicator and defined data element;
   - General and specific data collection instructions;
   - Sampling instructions; and
   - Place for documenting the time and date of data collection and the data collector's name.

continued on next page

Worksheet #9. Data Management Plan (continued)

5. Identify any data quality control issues and how they will be addressed (for example, data completeness, data accuracy, and so forth).

   _____

   _____

   _____

6. Briefly describe the data collectors.

   _____

   _____

   _____

7. Briefly describe any necessary data collection training that will be provided.

   _____

   _____

   _____

PART II.   Preparing For Data Analysis

Describe how data will be analyzed.

Consider the following _quantitative_ strategies:
- Descriptive statistics (averages, percentages, rates, ratios, and so on);
- Variation statistics (standard deviation, ANOVA, data runs, control charts, and so on);
- Capability statistics; and
- Relationship statistics (correlations, regression analyses, and so on).

Consider the following _qualitative_ strategies:
- Content analysis for key concepts; and
- Theme analysis for patterns.

Consider the following _comparative analysis_ strategies:
- Time series studies;
- Comparisons of matched, discrete time periods; and
- Benchmarking. (Specify benchmarking sources and "best practice" performance targets.)

Consider the following _root cause analysis_ strategies:
- Process flow diagram;
- Cause-effect diagram;
- Scatter diagram;
- Pareto analysis; and
- Repetitive Why?

continued on next page

Worksheet #9. Data Management Plan (continued)

PART III. Action Plan For Pilot Testing Data Collection And Data Analysis

Complete the following action plan, detailing each step in the pilot testing of the data collection and analysis processes.

ACTION STEP	RESPONSIBLE PERSON	DATE DUE
Data Collection:		

Data Analysis:

PART IV. Data Management Time Line

Fill in the projected dates for completing each milestone when developing the data management plan. After accomplishing each milestone, document the actual date of completion.

MILESTONE	PROJECTED DATE	ACTUAL DATE
1. Sample drawn.	_____	_____
2. Data collection tool developed.	_____	_____
3. Training of data collectors completed.	_____	_____
4. Data analysis strategies determined.	_____	_____
5. Initiation of pilot test.	_____	_____
6. Completion of pilot test.	_____	_____
7. Data collection started.	_____	_____
8. Data collection completed.	_____	_____
9. Data analysis started.	_____	_____
10. Data analysis completed.	_____	_____

Worksheet #10. Improvement Team Final Report

Team Name: _____

Date Team Was Assigned: _____

Date of Final Team Report and Recommendations: _____

Team Membership:

Executive
Sponsor: _____ Leader: _____

Facilitator: _____

Members: _____ _____

_____ _____

_____ _____

_____ _____

Ex-Officio
Members: _____ _____

_____ _____

Summary of the Team's Work: (Briefly describe the process the team used to prepare for data collection, collect data, analyze data, generate improvement ideas, and prepare the final report.)

_____
_____
_____

Analysis of Causes for Current Performance: (Describe, in detail, the data that were collected and the collection process, how the data were analyzed, and the results of the data analysis. Attach graphs and charts, as necessary.) _____

_____
_____
_____

Recommended Improvement Actions: (Rank order from most important to least important.)

_____
_____
_____

Test Plan for Improvement # :_____
(Create a separate test plan for every improvement idea.)

1. Propose how the improvement idea can be tested on a small scale. Identify who will need to be involved in the test. Describe any staff education that will be needed in order to test the improvement idea. Describe any other support needs or changes that must be made in order to test the improvement idea. Indicate where and when the test could occur. _____

_____
_____

2. Describe how the tested improvement idea will be evaluated. Specify what measures should be used to determine if the change is an improvement. Identify who could collect the performance data, how it will be collected, and how it will be analyzed._____

_____
_____

3. Specify any anticipated issues or problems with conducting the test _____

_____
_____

Glossary

Administrative/Financial Measure: A measure that addresses the organization structure for coordinating and integrating services, functions, or activities across operational components, including financial management (for example, financial stability, utilization/length of stay, credentials review).

Aggregated Measurement Data: Measurement data collected and reported by organizations as a sum or total over a given time period (for example, monthly, quarterly) or for certain groupings (for example, health care organization level).

Assess: Transforming data into information by analyzing it.

Assessment: The systematic collection and review of data. Assessment of performance data examines performance over time and in comparison to other referents.

Benchmarking: The process of comparing one organization's processes and outcomes with another organization's processes and outcomes or with the process and outcomes data captured in a reference database.

Clinical Measure: A measure designed to evaluate the processes or outcomes of care associated with the *delivery of clinical services*. It allows for the use of intra- and interorganization comparisons to continuously improve patient health outcomes. It may focus on the appropriateness of clinical decision making and implementation of these decisions. It must be condition specific, procedure specific, or address important functions of patient care (such as medication use, infection control, patient assessment, and so on).

Common Cause Variation: The random variation inherent in all work processes. Reduction or elimination of common cause variation requires an assessment and redesign of the targeted processes. When statistical analysis demonstrates only common cause variation in processes or outcomes, those processes or outcomes are said to be stable. (It is important to note that *stable* is not equal to *good* or *bad*. It simply means that there is no special cause variation in the system.)

Data: Uninterpreted material, facts, or clinical observations. Data may be numeric or quantitative. Examples of quantitative data include

■ creatinine and BUN in patients pre- and postdialysis;

■ oxygen saturation rate in patients undergoing gastroesophagoduodenoscopy; and

■ average number of visits to the student health center each semester.

Data may also be non-numeric or qualitative, reflecting the "lived experience" of the population of interest. Examples of qualitative data include

■ perceived benefit of chiropractic treatment in increasing flexibility and mobility and reducing pain in patients with neck and shoulder symptoms;

■ dysphagia experienced by individuals undergoing head and neck radiation; and

■ patients' experience of empathy and attentiveness of care providers in a women's health center.

Database: An organized, comprehensive collection of data elements (variables) and their values.

Data Collection: The act or process of capturing raw or primary data from a single or number of sources. Also called "data gathering."

Data Collection Tool: A user-friendly composite of indicators, trigger questions, or statements aimed at eliciting performance data about specific issues of concern.

Data Element: A discrete piece of data, such as patient birth date or principal diagnosis.

Data Reliability: The stability, repeatability, or precision of data.

Data Validity: Verification of correctness; reflects the true situation.

Financial Measure: A measure that addresses an organization's fiscal performance.

Function: A goal-directed, interrelated series of processes, such as continuum of care or management of information.

Health Status Measures: Measures that address changes in functional well-being of specific populations. They may address general health or specific health conditions.

Indicator: Also known as *performance measure.* A measure used to determine an organization's performance of functions, processes, and outcomes over time.

Information: Interpreted set(s) of data that can assist in decision making.

Measure: To collect quantifiable data about a function or process.

Measurement: The systematic process of data collection, repeated over time or at a single point in time.

ORYX (ORYX Outcomes: The Next Evolution in Accreditation): A performance measurement initiative of the Joint Commission which is intended to be a flexible and affordable approach to progressively increasing the relevance of accreditation, and an important building block for supporting quality improvement efforts in accredited organizations.

Outcome: The result of the performance (or non-performance) of a function or process.

Outcomes Measure: A measure that indicates the result of the performance or non-performance of a function or process.

Outcomes Measurement: The collection and analysis of data about the result(s) of implementing one or more processes.

Perception of Care and Services Measures: Satisfaction measures that focus on one or more aspects of care from the patient's/family's/caregiver's perspective. These include, but are not limited to, patient education, medication use, pain management, communication regarding plans and outcomes of care, prevention of illness, improvement in health status, and so forth.

Performance: The way in which an individual, group, or organization carries out or accomplishes its important functions.

Performance Improvement: The continuous study and adaptation of a health care organization's functions and processes to increase the probability of achieving desired outcomes and to better meet the needs of individuals and other users of services. This is the third segment of a performance measurement, assessment, and improvement system.

Performance Improvement Plan: A documented description of an organization's chosen approach to identifying and achieving performance improvement goals. Often, the performance improvement plan contains a section that is dedicated to performance measurement. Typically, this section includes

- a description of how the organization will implement performance measurement activities;

- the specification of critical outcomes and processes that will be measured in an ongoing fashion;

- a protocol for conducting non-routine performance measurement activities; and

- a summary of the format, content, distribution frequency, and audience of performance reports.

Performance Measure: A tool that provides an indication of an organization's performance in relation to a specified process or outcome. A performance measure is sometimes called an indicator. Performance measures, or indicators, are the fundamental building blocks of a performance measurement system.

Performance Measurement System: An entity consisting of an automated database that facilitates performance improvement in health care organizations through the collection and dissemination of process and outcomes measures of performance. Measurement systems must be able to generate internal comparisons of organization performance over time and external comparisons of performance among participating organizations at comparable times.

Process: A series of goal-directed, interdependent actions, decisions, judgments, or events. Processes may be clinical or nonclinical.

Process Measure: A performance measure that is used to assess the operations of goal-directed, interrelated series of actions, events, mechanisms, or steps.

Process Measurement: The collection and analysis of data about the performance or operations of key processes.

Reference Database: An organized collection of similar data from many organizations that can be used to compare an organization's performance to that of others.

Relevance: The pertinence and/or applicability of a measure, from the perspective of the data user(s) and customer(s).

Reliability: The ability of the indicator to accurately and consistently identify the events it was designed to identify across multiple health care settings.

Risk Adjustment: A statistical method for reducing, removing, or clarifying the effect of confounding factors that contribute to clinical outcomes and differ among comparison groups. It is used to make cross-comparisons more meaningful when there are differences in health factors of the samples or populations being compared. Risk adjustment in ambulatory care is still in the early stages. Significantly more work is needed to identify and account for a broad spectrum of factors that affect outcomes.

Satisfaction Measures: Measures that evaluate how well patients, enrollees, practitioners, purchasers, payers and other vested parties perceive their needs are met.

Sentinel Event: A sentinel event is an unexpected occurrence involving death or serious physical or psychological injury, or risk thereof. Serious injury specifically includes loss of limb

or function. The phrase "or the risk thereof" includes any process variation for which a recurrence would carry a significant chance of a serious adverse outcome.

Special Cause Variation: The fluctuation or differences in processes or outcomes that is not attributable to random variation. It is assignable to a specific cause or causes that are not an inherent part of the targeted work process. Special cause variation may result in either desirable or undesirable events. When statistical analysis demonstrates the presence of special cause variation in processes or outcomes, those processes or outcomes are said to be unstable. (It is important to note that *unstable* is not equal to *good* or *bad*. It simply means that there is special cause variation in the system.)

Structure: Those elemental aspects of service delivery (such as the number, type, and distribution of staff, equipment, supplies, and facilities) that must be present for care to be delivered. In a very real sense, an organization's ability to operate is contingent upon the adequacy of its structures. If key structures are missing or inadequate, the essential care and administrative processes will not operate effectively or efficiently and desired outcomes may be achieved sporadically or not at all.

Structure Measure: A measure of whether organization resources and arrangements are in place to deliver health care.

Utilization Management: A planned and systematic approach to identifying, defining, and evaluating the use of an organization's resources, in service of providing the most efficacious and appropriate health care for the least cost. Both the direct and indirect costs of providing health services and interventions are now commonly recognized as outcomes of the clinical care process. Tracking, trending, and cumulating resources consumed as a consequence of providing care will continue to be one of the most essential outcomes measurement activities that an ambulatory care organization can conduct.

Validity: Ability to identify opportunities for improvement in the quality of care; demonstration that the indicator use results in improvements in outcomes and/or quality of care.

Value: A judgment made by a customer based on the intersection of cost and quality. Value addresses the question: "Is this health care product worth what I'm being asked to pay for it?"

Variance: A measure of the differences in a set of observations.

Variation: The fluctuation or difference in process performance and outcomes. Sources of variation in health care include patient factors, practitioner factors, organization factors, factors related to the external environment, and chance. Two distinct types of variation exist: common cause and special cause.

Index

Note: Page numbers followed by *f* indicate figures. Page numbers followed by *t* indicate tables.